IN THE RAYS OF LIGHT

LIVING THE QURAN
THROUGH
THE LIVING QURAN

SURAH YASEEN

THE HEART OF THE QURAN

Written by Shaykh Muḥsin Qarāʾatī
Translated by Saleem Bhimji

Edited by Arifa Hudda

ISBN 978-1-927930-67-0

Commentary of Surah Yaseen
A Translation from *Tafsīr-e Nūr*
Written by Shaykh Muḥsin Qarāʾatī

Translated by Saleem Bhimji
Edited by Arifa Hudda

Cover Design and Layout by Saleem Bhimji

Published by Islamic Publishing House

www.iph.ca · iph@iph.ca

Contents

بسم الله الرحمن الرحيم

In the Name of Allah,
the All-Compassionate,
the All-Merciful

Foreword by the Translator

From the multitudes of commentaries *(tafāsīr)* that have been written by Muslim scholars over the past 12 centuries in their attempts to better understand the Quran and make it relevant to the lives of everyday Muslims, the present work of Shaykh Muḥsin Qarā'atī, *Tafsīr-e Nūr* – The Exegesis of Light, is a unique attempt to bring the Quran into the homes of all of humanity.

Although sometimes very brief in his explanation, Shaykh Muḥsin makes up for the brevity of the commentary by providing the reader with **Take Away Messages**. These detailed points guide the readers to key pieces of guidance on how to make the Quran relevant to their daily lives – thus, being able to *Live the Quran Through the Living Quran.*

We hope and pray that the translation and publication of this commentary serves to bridge the great divide which has existed within the Muslim community for generations and allows them to benefit from the beautiful teachings of the Noble Quran in their daily lives.

The initial project to translate *Tafsīr-e Nūr* into English was envisioned in early 2018 and was initially meant to strictly be a podcast rendition of the translation.

However, due to popular demand and the support of well-wishers around the world, we expanded the scope of this project to release the PDF of the commentary of each chapter of the Quran as we completed them.

With the advancement in Print-On-Demand services globally, we have taken it a step further and decided to release the translation of the commentary of each chapter in print version.

Most commentaries of the Quran are published with each volume consisting of hundreds of pages, and this often puts some people off from wanting to try and understand the Quran. It is our hope that by publishing the commentary of the Quran in the format we have chosen – that is, chapter by chapter – readers will be encouraged to pick up the exegesis of the chapter that interests them the most. In this way, over time, they will have read the commentary of the entire Quran, gaining inspiration from its teachings.

As we present this work to our readers, we are deeply grateful to all of those who have made it possible.

We extend our heartfelt thanks to our editor, Sr. Arifa Hudda, whose tireless dedication, and expertise have been instrumental in bringing this project to fruition. For almost 25 years, Sr. Arifa has been a cornerstone of the Islamic Publishing House, guiding our publications with her keen insight and unwavering commitment to excellence. Her contribution to this work, as with all our publications, has been invaluable.

We would like to thank those donors who financially contributed towards the publishing of this book, as well as the other books in this series, and we ask you to recite a Sūrah al-Fātiḥa for their rewards and their dearly departed loved ones *(marhūmīn)*.

We are also profoundly grateful to our well-wishers, whose generous support – in many ways – enabled us to undertake this ambitious project. Their belief in the importance of the Quran, and their commitment to fostering a deeper understanding of the Book of Allah within our community have been a constant source of inspiration and encouragement.

In closing, if you would like to support this project by sponsoring its publication, either individually or with your family, friends, and community members, choose a chapter of the Quran that you would like to see published, and contact us at iph@iph.ca for more information.

In conclusion, we pray to Allah ﷻ to accept the translation of this brief, yet unique look into Sūrah Yāsīn, and that we can spread the beautiful teachings of Allah ﷻ through *Living the Quran Through the Living Quran.*

Saleem Bhimji
Director *of the* Islamic Publishing House
August 1st, 2025 CE ♦ 7th of Safar, 1447 AH
Martyrdom of Imam Ḥasan ibn ʿAlī al-Mujtaba ؑ
Kitchener, ON, Canada

سُورَةُ يسٓ

An Introduction to Sūrah Yāsīn[1]

Sūrah Yāsīn was revealed in the city of Mecca, or better yet, during the Meccan era of the life of Prophet Muḥammad ﷺ. Therefore, its contents are related to what is generally seen in other chapters revealed in that period – themes such as Monotheism *(Tawḥīd)*, Resurrection *(Maʿād)*, the revelation of the Quran, and the warnings and glad-tidings given to humanity, and some other areas, which we will see as we delve into the commentary of this chapter.

Specifics of this Chapter

This chapter covers the following areas:

1. It begins by speaking about the Prophethood of the final Messenger, Prophet Muḥammad ﷺ, as well as the Noble Quran, and one of the goals for why this Heavenly-sent Book was revealed.
2. Another portion of this chapter covers three individuals who were sent by Allah ﷻ as Prophets for a community. The verses speak about how they carried out their mission of inviting others towards Monotheism, how they struggled against the idol worshippers, as well as the resolve they showed in opposing polytheism. This story may have been told to Prophet Muḥammad ﷺ at a

[1] Extracted from *Tafsīr-e Nemunah* – written by His Eminence, Āyatullāh Shaykh Nāṣir Makārim Shīrāzī.

particular juncture in Mecca as a form of consolation to him, and to direct him to the best path to follow to fulfill his critical responsibility of guiding his community, and society in general.

3. The next portion of this chapter, from verses 33 until 44, is rich in interesting points regarding Monotheism, and profound arguments regarding the Greatness of Allah ﷻ and His magnificent signs – as can be seen in the physical world.
4. The next, and perhaps most important, aspect of this chapter focuses on:
    a. The resurrection and various proofs for its occurrence.
    b. The method by which humanity will be brought back to life and gathered for the accounting of their deeds.
    c. The questioning of people by Allah ﷻ on the Day of Judgement.
    d. The end of this present world.
    e. Some scenes of Paradise and Hell.
5. The final portion contains extremely crucial, unique, and meticulously worded discussions on the world to come.

The verses contained in Sūrah Yāsīn will move the soul and awaken those who are in a state of spiritual heedlessness.

In short, the person who engages in careful, contemplative reading and reflection of this chapter will come face to face with various scenes of their own personal existence.

It all starts from their creation, moving on to life in this world, and finally their eventual death and resurrection. Through this journey, the readers will come across verses which highlight the warnings and glad tidings of Allah ﷻ, and much more. Ultimately, all of this is for one goal: to awaken the conscience and act as a prescription to reform the self before it is too late.

Merits of Recitation

According to multiple *aḥādīth* which speak about Sūrah Yāsīn, we are told that this is one of the most important chapters of the Quran, and the traditions refer to it as the "Heart of the Quran." For example, the Noble Prophet ﷺ has been quoted as saying: "Everything has a heart, and the heart of the Quran is [Sūrah] Yāsīn."[2]

In a lengthy *ḥadīth* from Imam al-Ṣādiq (ع), he has been quoted as saying: "Indeed, everything has a heart, and the heart of the Quran is Sūrah Yāsīn.

A person who recites it before going to bed, or any part of the day, will remain safe during that day and will receive blessings from Allah. One who recites it before going to bed at night, Almighty Allah will appoint seventy angels to protect them from the mischief of Satan and all sorts of calamities.

If they die the next day, Allah will allow them to enter Paradise, and 30,000 angels will be present at the time of the ritual bathing *(Ghusl al-Mayyit)* of their body.

---

[2] ʿAllāmah Ṭabrisī, *Tafsīr Majmaʿ al-Bayān*. The Arabic text of this tradition is as follows:

إِنَّ لِكُلِّ شَيْءٍ قَلْبًا وَإِنَّ قَلْبَ الْقُرْآنِ يٰسٓ.

The angels will repent on their behalf and pray for their forgiveness and accompany them until their burial in the grave.

They [the angels] will enter the grave before the person is laid in it and worship [Allah] there, and the reward of this worship will be given to the deceased.

The grave will be expanded for a distance as far as the eyes can see, and the person will remain safe from the squeezing of the grave, and an illuminated light will emerge from their grave stretching into the heavens, and this light will remain until the time when Allah orders for them to be taken out of their grave [on the Day of Resurrection].

When they are resurrected from the grave, they will be speaking to the angels, and their face will be resplendent.

The angels will give them good news at every stage until they pass over the bridge *(ṣirāṭ)* and pass through the scale *(mīzān)*. They [the angels] will take the person so near to Allah that no one except the nearest angels and Prophets have been there.

This individual will stand in front of Allah with the Prophets [in their midst], and while others will be sorrowful and troubled, this person will have no sorrow, trouble, or difficulties.

[At this stage] Allah will say to that person: 'Intercede for whomsoever you want – I will accept your intercession; and ask whatever you want – for I will grant it to you.'

This person will get whatever they desire, and if they do intercede for anyone, it will be accepted, while others will have to give account of their deeds. Others will be stopped and disgraced, but there will be no accounting for this person.

No one will stop them, and there will be no disgrace for them; they will not face any bad fortune for their deeds, and their scroll of deeds will be opened and given to them.

When they return after meeting Allah, people will say: 'Glory be to Allah' *(Subḥān Allah)* upon seeing them, and in return, they will respond: 'There is no sin attached to the name of this servant,' and from this point forward, they will be in the company of Muḥammad.'"[3]

---

[3] *Tafsīr Majma' al-Bayān.* The Arabic text of this tradition is as follows:

إِنَّ لِكُلِّ شَيْءٍ قَلْبًا وَإِنَّ قَلْبَ الْقُرْآنِ يٰسٓ وَمَنْ قَرَأَهَا قَبْلَ أَنْ يَنَامَ أَوْ فِي نَهَارِهِ قَبْلَ أَنْ يَمْشِيَ كَانَ فِي نَهَارِهِ مِنَ الْمَحْفُوظِينَ وَالْمَرْزُوقِينَ حَتَّى يُمْسِيَ. وَمَنْ قَرَأَهَا فِي لَيْلِهِ قَبْلَ أَنْ يَنَامَ وَكَّلَ اللّٰهُ بِهِ أَلْفَ مَلَكٍ يَحْفَظُونَهُ مِنْ شَرِّ كُلِّ شَيْطَانٍ رَجِيمٍ وَمِنْ كُلِّ آفَةٍ. وَإِنْ مَاتَ فِي يَوْمِهِ أَدْخَلَهُ اللّٰهُ الْجَنَّةَ وَحَضَرَ غُسْلَهُ ثَلَاثُونَ أَلْفَ مَلَكٍ كُلُّهُمْ يَسْتَغْفِرُونَ لَهُ وَيُشَيِّعُونَهُ إِلَى قَبْرِهِ بِالاسْتِغْفَارِ لَهُ. فَإِذَا دَخَلَ فِي لَحْدِهِ كَانُوا فِي جَوْفِ قَبْرِهِ يَعْبُدُونَ اللّٰهَ وَثَوَابُ عِبَادَتِهِمْ لَهُ وَفُسِّحَ لَهُ فِي قَبْرِهِ مَدَّ بَصَرِهِ وَأُومِنَ مِنْ ضَغْطَةِ الْقَبْرِ وَلَمْ يَزَلْ لَهُ فِي قَبْرِهِ نُورٌ سَاطِعٌ إِلَى عَنَانِ السَّمَاءِ إِلَى أَنْ يُخْرِجَهُ اللّٰهُ مِنْ قَبْرِهِ فَإِذَا أَخْرَجَهُ لَمْ تَزَلْ مَلَائِكَةُ اللّٰهِ يُشَيِّعُونَهُ وَيُحَدِّثُونَهُ وَيَضْحَكُونَ فِي وَجْهِهِ وَيُبَشِّرُونَهُ بِكُلِّ خَيْرٍ حَتَّى يُجَوِّزُونَهُ عَلَى الصِّرَاطِ وَالْمِيزَانِ وَيُوقِفُونَهُ مِنَ اللّٰهِ مَوْقِفًا لَا يَكُونُ عِنْدَ اللّٰهِ خَلْقًا أَقْرَبَ مِنْهُ إِلَّا مَلَائِكَةُ اللّٰهِ الْمُقَرَّبُونَ وَأَنْبِيَاؤُهُ الْمُرْسَلُونَ وَهُوَ مَعَ النَّبِيِّينَ وَاقِفٌ بَيْنَ يَدَيِ اللّٰهِ لَا يَحْزَنُ مَعَ مَنْ يَحْزَنُ وَلَا يَهُمُّ مَعَ مَنْ يَهُمُّ وَلَا يَجْزَعُ مَعَ مَنْ يَجْزَعُ ثُمَّ يَقُولُ لَهُ الرَّبُّ تَبَارَكَ وَتَعَالَى اشْفَعْ عَبْدِي أُشَفِّعْكَ فِي جَمِيعِ مَا تَشْفَعُ وَسَلْنِي أُعْطِكَ عَبْدِي جَمِيعَ مَا تَسْأَلُ فَيَسْأَلُ فَيُعْطَى وَيَشْفَعُ وَلَا يُحَاسَبُ فِيمَنْ يُحَاسَبُ وَلَا يُوقَفُ مَعَ مَنْ يُوقَفُ وَلَا يَذِلُّ مَعَ مَنْ يَذِلُّ وَلَا

In addition, there is tradition from Prophet Muḥammad ﷺ in which he has been quoted as saying: "[The contents of] Sūrah Yāsīn has been referred to in the Tawrāh as the 'General Acclamation' *(Al-Miʿammah)* as it will grant the person (who is close to this chapter through its recitation and application) all of the goodness of this world and the world to come; and it will divert the difficulties of this world and the world to come from such a person; and it will repel the fears of the world to come.

This [chapter] is also known as The Repeller *(Al-Dāfiʿah)* and The Judge *(Al-Qāḍiah)*, and it will drive away from the person (who is close to this chapter through its recitation and application) all evil, and it will aide in the fulfilment of every legitimate desire (they have).

The person who recites it will receive a reward which is equivalent to the performance of twenty *Ḥajj* (pilgrimages to Mecca).

The person who hears it being recited will be rewarded as if they gave one thousand *dīnār*[4] in charity in the Way of Allah.

A person who writes this sūrah (for example with saffron and water), then drinks the writing will find that this mixture

---

يُكْتَبُ بِخَطِيئَةٍ وَلَا بِشَيْءٍ مِنْ سُوءِ عَمَلِهِ وَيُعْطَى كِتَابًا مَنْشُورًا حَتَّى يَهْبِطَ مِنْ عِنْدِ اللهِ فَيَقُولُ النَّاسُ بِأَجْمَعِهِمْ سُبْحَانَ اللهِ مَا كَانَ لِهٰذَا الْعَبْدِ مِنْ خَطِيئَةٍ وَاحِدَةٍ وَيَكُونُ مِنْ رُفَقَاءِ مُحَمَّدٍ.

[4] In traditional Muslim/Arab societies, the *dīnār* is a gold coin, while the *dirham* is a silver coin, and were legal tenders.

will be the infusion of one thousand medicines, one thousand light *(nūr)*, one thousand stages of certainty *(yaqīn)*, one thousand blessings *(barakāt)*, and one thousand mercies *(raḥmah)*; and all forms of hatred and illness will be kept away from this person."[5]

There are many more traditions in the books of the Shīʿa and Ahlul Sunnah regarding the importance of Sūrah Yāsīn, however, if we were to mention all of them, then this discussion would become very lengthy.

Thus, from these few traditions we have quoted, and the bulk which remain in the books of *aḥādīth*, we must recognize that there is perhaps no other chapter of the Quran which has so much importance attributed to it by the Prophet of Islam ﷺ than this sūrah.

However, we should recognize that the immense rewards which are recorded in the *aḥādīth* for reciting this chapter are not simply given for the mere verbalization of this chapter. Rather, the greatness of this chapter and its merits are due to

---

[5] ʿĀmilī, Muḥammad ibn al-Ḥasan al-, *Wasāʾil al-Shīʿa*, Vol. 4, Pg. 886. The Arabic text of this tradition is as follows:

سُورَةُ يٰسٓ تُدْعَى فِي التَّوْرَاةِ الْمِعَمَّةَ تَعُمُّ صَاحِبَهَا بِخَيْرِ الدُّنْيَا وَالْآخِرَةِ وَتُكَابِدُ عَنْهُ بَلْوَى الدُّنْيَا وَالْآخِرَةِ وَتَدْفَعُ عَنْهُ أَهَاوِيلَ الْآخِرَةِ وَتُسَمَّى الدَّافِعَةَ وَالْقَاضِيَةَ وَتَدْفَعُ عَنْ صَاحِبِهَا كُلَّ سُوءٍ وَتَقْضِي لَهُ كُلَّ حَاجَةٍ مَنْ قَرَأَهَا عَدَلَتْ لَهُ عِشْرِينَ حَجَّةً وَمَنْ سَمِعَهَا عَدَلَتْ لَهُ أَلْفَ دِينَارٍ فِي سَبِيلِ اللّٰهِ وَمَنْ كَتَبَهَا ثُمَّ شَرِبَهَا أَدْخَلَتْ جَوْفَهُ أَلْفَ دَوَاءٍ وَأَلْفَ نُورٍ وَأَلْفَ يَقِينٍ وَأَلْفَ بَرَكَةٍ وَأَلْفَ رَحْمَةٍ وَنَزَعَتْ عَنْهُ كُلَّ غِلٍّ وَدَاءٍ.

the unique contents within it, which we must learn and take lessons from, and implement in our lives.

The contents of Sūrah Yāsīn are meant to awaken an individual, stir their faith, make them recognize their great responsibility, and increase in their God-consciousness *(taqwā)*. Indeed, all of this can only take place when a person reflects on the matters discussed in this sūrah and then acts according to the teachings of this chapter. It is only at that time that a person will be worthy of and be able to pave the way for the goodness of this world and the world to come.

For example, in verse seventy of this chapter, we will read that there was a pledge taken by Allah ﷻ with humanity that they would not submit to the orders of the Devil as he is introduced as their open enemy. Any time a human being stays loyal to this covenant, then just as the above quoted *aḥādīth* have stated, they will be safe and protected from the accursed Satan. However, if a believer continuously reads this verse of Sūrah Yāsīn, but remains a sincere and committed friend of the Devil by following his insinuations and knowingly engages in sin, then they will be deprived of the blessings which this chapter has to offer – and this goes for each verse of Sūrah Yāsīn, as well as all of the other chapters of the Quran.

May Allah ﷻ allow us all to read, reflect, and implement the beautiful teachings contained in this chapter.

Part 1: You Are on the Straight Path – Verses 1-4

بِسْمِ ٱللَّهِ ٱلرَّحْمَٰنِ ٱلرَّحِيمِ

In the Name of Allah, the All-Compassionate, the All-Merciful.

يسٓ ۝١ وَٱلْقُرْءَانِ ٱلْحَكِيمِ ۝٢ إِنَّكَ لَمِنَ ٱلْمُرْسَلِينَ ۝٣ عَلَىٰ صِرَٰطٍ مُّسْتَقِيمٍ ۝٤

1. Yā Sīn.
2. (I take an oath) By the Quran, which is full of wisdom,
3. (That) Indeed, you (O Muḥammad) are from among the Messengers,
4. On the Straight (and Right) Path.

Thinking Points

According to the traditions, Yāsīn is one of the blessed names of Prophet Muḥammad ﷺ.[6]

The word "*al-ḥakīm*" can be taken to mean 'that which possesses wisdom' *(dhūl ḥikmah)*, or it can also be taken as meaning 'wise' *(ḥakīm)*.

The Straight Path *(Ṣirāṭ al-Mustaqīm)* is not a path like those in this temporal world such that after covering its distance, an individual will reach the goal. Rather, to the extent that one travels The Straight Path *(Ṣirāṭ al-Mustaqīm)*,

---

[6] *Tafsīr Majmaʿ al-Bayān.*

they will reach a part of the destination. The prime example of how this works is that of studying – no matter how much a person goes down the path of learning, one will reach to that specific level of knowledge according to how much they studied – but there will always be more to learn, and go down further on the path of knowledge.

In the face of the various types of slanders which were levelled against the Prophet ﷺ in which he was called a poet *(shāʿir)*, a magician *(kāhin)*, and ultimately that he was insane *(majnūn)*, Allah ﷻ, the All-Wise, swears by the wisdom of the Quran, and emphasizes the mission and truthfulness of the final Messenger of Islam ﷺ.

Take Away Messages

1. There is no falsehood in the Quran – it is unadulterated and reliable.
2. Taking an oath on the Quran, and that too by Allah ﷻ doing so, shows the greatness and sanctity of this Book.
3. It is imperative to protect the integrity of what is accurate and reliable in the face of attacks of false accusations and attempts to weaken the truth.
4. People chosen by Allah ﷻ to deliver messages to humanity are not isolated in history. Allah ﷻ sent a long chain of such individuals to guide people back to His path and teachings.
5. The path of the Prophets which Allah ﷻ sent for the guidance of humanity is the path of Allah ﷻ – just as we see in the Quran where Prophet Hūd عليه السلام has been

quoted as saying: "I have put my trust in Allah, my Lord, and your Lord. No living creature is there, but He holds it by its forelock and keeps it under His complete control. Surely, my Lord is on a Straight Path (He governs all that exists and carries out His decrees rightly and with absolute justice)."[7]

6. Three things are necessary to succeed in life:
    a. **A well-defined plan:** In this case, the blueprint of life must be the Wise Quran.
    b. **A teacher to instruct and show how to implement the plan:** That person must also be a wise leader, and this is Prophet Muḥammad ﷺ.
    c. **A clear, well-defined way to follow:** The Straight Path – this is none other than the combination of the theory based in the Quran, and the practical application of the Quran – the method of life of Prophet Muḥammad ﷺ and the immaculate Imams of the Ahlul Bayt عليهم السلام.
7. The foundation of belief must be unchangeable and wise. Allah ﷻ is the All-Wise *(al-Ḥakīm)*; the Quran is a Book replete with wisdom *(Ḥikmah)*; and Prophet Muḥammad ﷺ is a man of great wisdom *(Ḥakīm)*.

---

[7] Quran, Sūrah Hūd (11), Verse 56:

﴿إِنِّي تَوَكَّلْتُ عَلَى ٱللَّهِ رَبِّي وَرَبِّكُمۚ مَّا مِن دَآبَّةٍ إِلَّا هُوَ ءَاخِذُۢ بِنَاصِيَتِهَآۚ إِنَّ رَبِّي عَلَىٰ صِرَٰطٖ مُّسۡتَقِيمٖ ٥٦﴾

Part 2: The Quran and Past Generations – Verses 5-6

تَنزِيلَ ٱلْعَزِيزِ ٱلرَّحِيمِ ۝٥ لِتُنذِرَ قَوْمًا مَّآ أُنذِرَ ءَابَآؤُهُمْ فَهُمْ غَٰفِلُونَ ۝٦

5. (This Quran is) a revelation sent by the All-Mighty *(al-'Azīz)*, the All-Merciful *(al-Raḥīm)*.

6. So that you (Muḥammad ﷺ) may warn the people whose predecessors were not warned, thus they are heedless.

Thinking Points

The Quran refers to Allah ﷻ as the 'All-Mighty' (*al-'Azīz*) to show His Power, and that this Book, the Quran, can never be eliminated – just as Allah ﷻ is All-Mighty, so too His Book shares this trait. Since its revelation over 1,400 years ago, the Quran remains a continuous miracle, and there is no human force, no matter how great they claim to be, who can eradicate or successfully debate and defeat the Book of Allah ﷻ.

At the same time, Allah ﷻ refers to Himself as the 'All-Merciful' (*al-Raḥīm*) and this is to show us that His Mercy necessitates that He send us revelation and allow us to benefit from this life-giving Book – the Quran.

Some commentators of the Quran have noted that the two descriptions mentioned in the verses under review are opposite reactions – as it is possible that when it comes to the revelation of the Quran, people would have one of the following reactions to the Messenger of Allah ﷺ:

1. If they want to oppose the verses of Allah ﷻ in the Quran, then Allah ﷻ is taking an oath by His Greatness, and the fact that He is All-Powerful *(al-ʿAzīz)* and He will deal with them – based on this trait of His.
2. If they listen, accept, and submit to the Words of the Quran, then Allah ﷻ will deal with them with His Mercy *(al-Raḥīm)*.[8]

Therefore, the Might and Mercy of Allah ﷻ which represent the traits of a display of the warning of Hell, and the glad tidings of Paradise are merged into one; and this Divinely sent Book, the Quran, which has been given to humanity, will allow them to choose which path they want to benefit from.

At this point, a question may come into the minds of the readers: Are we able to reinforce the authenticity of a Prophet sent by Allah ﷻ or a Book which claims to have come from Allah ﷻ through such statements?

The response to this question is contained within these verses.

From one angle, by Allah ﷻ referring to the Quran as having been sent by One who is All-Wise *(al-Ḥakīm)* points us to the fact that its verses are full of wisdom for all to experience – and thus, its contents itself point to its truthfulness without requiring any external source. One needs to simply study the Quran – having removed all pre-

---

[8] Fakhr al-Dīn al-Rāzī, *Mafātīḥ al-Ghayb* (also known as *Tafsīr al-Kabīr*).

conceived prejudices from their mind – and at the same time, keep in mind the history of the pre-Islamic Arabs as they read such verses which were being revealed during their time.

From another perspective, by the Quran describing the Noble Prophet ﷺ as being on the Straight Path *(Ṣirāṭ al-Mustaqīm)*, this shows us that his invitation guides the person who follows him to the Straight Path as well.

In addition, by studying the lifestyle *(Sunnah)* of Prophet Muḥammad ﷺ, we realize that he follows nothing but a clear, Straight Path which leads to felicity in this world and the next.

In previous discussions (in the commentary of other parts of the Quran), we discussed the proofs of the realities of the invitations of the past Prophets sent by Allah ﷻ. However, one point we should mention here is that one of the best ways to realize the truthfulness of these men sent by Allah ﷻ for the guidance of humanity is to carefully study the content of their invitation and what they were calling to. Whenever the Prophets which Allah ﷻ sent guide us to something in line with human nature, intellect, and our conscience, and is something that is at such a level that is beyond the ability of other humans to create and present, then we must recognize it as coming from a Higher Source.

Keeping this point in mind, when we study the life of Prophet Muḥammad ﷺ, we see that he was a man known throughout his society of idolators as being truthful *(al-Ṣādiq)* and trustworthy *(al-Amīn)* – he was **not ever** known to be a liar, a cheater, or one who made up things. All these factors together, as well as many more, prove that he was sent by Allah ﷻ.

Thus, the verse under review shows us this reality, and therefore, the oaths which Allah ﷻ takes are not worthless or without any basis.

We can take this discussion a step further, and if we were to study the art of debate, we will see that to penetrate the hearts of those who deny Allah ﷻ, His Prophet ﷺ, and His teachings, the more the message is presented with decisiveness and determination and with extra emphasis, the more the listening party will be interested and influenced to reflect on what they are being told.

With all this said, there is one more question which people pose which we must answer: Why is the one being spoken to directly in these initial verses – Prophet Muḥammad ﷺ, and not the polytheists, nor the masses of people – Muslims or otherwise, as Allah ﷻ clearly says: "(That) Indeed, you (O Muḥammad ﷺ) are from among the Messengers, on the Straight Path."

The answer to this question is that Allah ﷻ has spoken in this way to provide the recipients of this message yet another layer of emphasis as to the importance of the Quran and its teachings. In essence, Allah ﷻ is saying: "You, O Muḥammad, are on the right way and Straight Path – whether these people accept you or reject you. For this reason, as you proceed in your weighty responsibility to convey the message, exert all your efforts, do not back down in the deliverance in any way, and never deviate from the true path – even though the detractors may not accept you or your invitation."

The next verse under review goes on to explain that at the primary level, the purpose of the revelation of the Quran was to warn the polytheist Arabs whose forefathers did not have a warner or messenger for generations, and thus, had sunk into the oblivions, would be warned and could make their way back to the One True God – Allah ﷻ.

Some may question that: As Muslims, we believe that no nation has ever been left without a warner and a guide, and that this Earth has never been devoid of a representative *(Ḥujjah)* of Allah ﷻ, so what is the correct way to understand this verse?

In response, we must realize that the Quran is alluding to a clear warner and a major Prophet to come from Allah ﷻ whose reputation and message spread throughout the lands – what we call a 'universal Messenger.' Otherwise, we do have a belief in our Theology that there must always be a Divinely appointed representative from Allah ﷻ at every time on Earth for those who are anxiously and eagerly seeking Him.

Although the period between the leaving of Prophet ʿIsā (عليه السلام) and the arrival of Prophet Muḥammad ﷺ is known as the period of *fatrah*,[9] this does not mean that there was

[9] This should not be confused with the Arabic term, *fiṭrah*, with the letter 't/ṭ' being the differentiator; and the vowel on the Arabic letter, *fā*. The latter (*fiṭrah* - فطرة) refers to the intrinsic human nature, while the former (*fatrah* – فترة) refers to the period between two Prophets sent by Allah ﷻ. See Quran: Sūrah al-Māʾidah (5), Verse 19:

﴿يَا أَهْلَ الْكِتَابِ قَدْ جَاءَكُمْ رَسُولُنَا يُبَيِّنُ لَكُمْ عَلَى **فَتْرَةٍ** مِنَ الرُّسُلِ أَنْ تَقُولُوا مَا جَاءَنَا مِنْ بَشِيرٍ وَلَا نَذِيرٍ. فَقَدْ جَاءَكُمْ بَشِيرٌ وَنَذِيرٌ. وَاللَّهُ عَلَى كُلِّ شَيْءٍ قَدِيرٌ ﴿١٩﴾﴾

absolutely no representative of Allah ﷻ upon the Earth for that almost 600-year period. Rather, the term ***fatrah*** refers to the fact that between Prophet ʿIsā ﵇ and Prophet Muḥammad ﷺ there was no 'major' Prophet sent by Allah ﷻ.

In this regard, the Commander of the Faithful, Imam ʿAlī ﵇, states that: "Indeed, Allah deputed Muḥammad at a time when there was not a single Arab who could read a book and claim to be a Prophet (sent by Allah ﷻ)."[10]

In any case, the purpose of the revelation of the Quran was to awaken the spiritually sleeping individuals, and make the heedless people aware of the dangers that surrounded them and the sins they had sunk into, and to pull them out of the polytheism and corruption which had polluted them. Concisely, the Quran is a basis of awareness and awakening, and the Book of purification of the heart and soul.[11]

"O People of the Book! Now, after a **long interlude** during which no Messengers have appeared, there has indeed come to you Our Messenger (Prophet Muḥammad ﷺ), making the whole truth clear to you, lest you should say: 'There has not come to us any bearer of good tidings, nor any warner.' Indeed, there has come to you a bearer of good tidings and a warner. And Allah has full Power over everything."

[10] *Nahj al-Balāgha*, Sermons 33 and 104:

إِنَّ اللّٰهَ بَعَثَ مُحَمَّدًا (صَلَّى اللّٰهُ عَلَيْهِ وَآلِهِ) وَلَيْسَ أَحَدٌ مِنَ الْعَرَبِ يَقْرَأُ كِتَابًا وَلَايَدَّعِي نُبُوَّةً.

[11] As *Tafsīr-e Nūr* had no commentary on this passage, we extracted and translated this portion from *Tafsīr-e Nemunah.*

Take Away Messages

1. Allah ﷻ is Merciful even with His opponents and those who deny Him – and if He were not, then He would not have sent messengers and guides to bring them to the Straight Path; however, when it comes to His friends – those who accept and follow Him, He is All-Merciful.

2. The Source of revelation of the Quran is the One who is the epitome of Strength and Mercy; thus, a person who takes hold of the Quran will reach a (special) station of respect, strength, and mercy.

3. Warning the people of impending punishment is one of the roles of the Prophets sent by Allah ﷻ.

4. Warning the masses is one of the techniques of Allah ﷻ *(Sunnatullāh)* – however, we see that people still fall into spiritual negligence *(ghaflah)* in their lives.

5. The foundation of preaching and warning people **must** be the teachings of the Quran.

6. The entire Quran is mercy – even the warnings which are contained within its verses stem from the mercy and care of Allah ﷻ over His creations.

Part 3: Self-Imposed Punishments – Verses 7-8

لَقَدْ حَقَّ ٱلْقَوْلُ عَلَىٰٓ أَكْثَرِهِمْ فَهُمْ لَا يُؤْمِنُونَ ۝٧ إِنَّا جَعَلْنَا فِىٓ
أَعْنَٰقِهِمْ أَغْلَٰلًا فَهِىَ إِلَى ٱلْأَذْقَانِ فَهُم مُّقْمَحُونَ ۝٨

7. Surely, most of them merit the sentence of Our punishment for they would not believe.

8. Indeed, We have put shackles around their necks, and they [the shackles] are (reaching right) up to their chins, so that they have become stiff-necked (due to their pride and false notions of superiority).

Thinking Points

In reviewing some of the key words in these verses, we must make note that the word *'adhqān'* is the plural of *'dhaqan,'* and it means the 'chin;' while the word *'muqmaḥūn'* is a word that is used in a common Arabic expression which denotes 'The camel lifted its head up.' Thus, by combining these words, this verse number eight means that just as when an animal, like a camel is given water to drink, if it does not want to drink any more water, it will lift its head up to signal that it is not thirsty, Allah ﷻ uses these words to symbolize that there are some people who when they are presented with the truths of the Divine revelation, they reject it, and metaphorically put their head up so as not to submit to the truth – showing their pride and arrogance.

The meaning of 'putting shackles around their necks' (as seen in verse eight) could be a reference to the punishment of the world to come, as it is mentioned in the Quran: "When the fetters and the chains shall be on their necks; they shall be dragged."[12] In addition, this verse may refer to the presence of superstitious beliefs which, just like heavy chains around their necks, weigh down the disbelieving polytheists, just as is seen in the Quran: "...and removes from them their burden and the shackles which were upon them..."[13]

Therefore, one of the responsibilities of the Prophets that Allah ﷻ sent for the guidance of humanity was that they struggled to remove the proverbial shackles and chains on the people – those of cultural backwardness, superstitions, and much more. However, some people did not want this freedom and preferred a life of subservience to their illogical cultural practices, and following the irrational ways of their ancestors.

'Al-qawl' has been translated in this verse as 'the word,' keeping in mind verse 13 of Sūrah al-Sajdah which states: "And if We had pleased, We could certainly have given to every soul its guidance, but the word *[al-qawl]* (which had

---

[12] Quran, Sūrah Ghāfir (40), Verse 71:

﴿إِذِ الْأَغْلَالُ فِي أَعْنَاقِهِمْ وَالسَّلَاسِلُ يُسْحَبُونَ﴾

[13] Quran, Sūrah al-Aʿrāf (7), Verse 157:

﴿وَيَضَعُ عَنْهُمْ إِصْرَهُمْ وَالْأَغْلَالَ الَّتِي كَانَتْ عَلَيْهِمْ﴾

gone forth) from Me was true: I will certainly fill Hell with the *jinn* and people all together."[14]

Thus, this meaning of 'word' is not the literal definition, but rather, it refers to the 'command of Allah ﷻ' which has been given regarding the punishment for those who follow something other than the Straight Path.

Take Away Messages

1. In every era, a large segment of society is in a state of spiritual heedlessness *(ghaflah)* and have no inclination for the truth – they prefer to live their lives oblivious of Allah ﷻ and His teachings.
2. Those who are in opposition to the truth must not discourage those who are working to propagate the faith. They may not want to believe in Allah ﷻ and His teachings; however, they must not be an impediment for those who are desperately seeking connection to the Creator and Maintainer of everything.
3. Spiritual negligence is the planting ground for disbelief – it begins with a person – whether they were born into a family of believers or a family of non-believers. If a person becomes actively inattentive to Allah ﷻ, then eventually their distancing themselves from acts of

[14] Quran, Sūrah al-Sajdah (32), Verse 13:

﴿وَلَوْ شِئْنَا لَآتَيْنَا كُلَّ نَفْسٍ هُدَاهَا وَلَـٰكِنْ حَقَّ الْقَوْلُ مِنِّي لَأَمْلَأَنَّ جَهَنَّمَ مِنَ الْجِنَّةِ وَالنَّاسِ أَجْمَعِينَ﴾

worship will lead towards spiritual negligence, and from there, to disbelief *(kufr).*

4. Although the eighth verse of Sūrah Yāsīn states that Allah ﷻ has placed shackles upon the necks of the disbelievers, it must be noted that the disbelievers themselves provided the foundation for the shackles to be imposed through their evil actions. We must never think that Allah ﷻ initiated the process of blocking people from the truth, then imposed these chains upon them [as that would go against the Justice of Allah ﷻ].

Part 4: Barriers and Impediments – Verse 9

وَجَعَلْنَا مِنۢ بَيْنِ أَيْدِيهِمْ سَدًّا وَمِنْ خَلْفِهِمْ سَدًّا فَأَغْشَيْنَٰهُمْ فَهُمْ لَا يُبْصِرُونَ ﴿٩﴾

9. And We have placed barriers in front of them, and barriers behind them, and covered them, so they do not see.

Thinking Points

The Quran is unwavering in its messages; it is also full of wisdom and is a Book which actively teaches and guides those who wish to be inspired by its contents. In addition, the message of Prophet Muḥammad ﷺ is definitive; and the path which religion guides towards has been outlined, and a follower of it will not deviate. Above all, the One who has set this entire process in motion, Allah ﷻ, is All-Mighty and All-Powerful.

However, since most people are unaware of the realities of religion, do not believe in God, or are overwhelmed with superstitious beliefs from their own culture or faith, whichever direction they go, their destination will end up being a dead end.

In this verse under review, Allah ﷻ refers to people who are extremely stubborn, and it is interesting how the Quran refers to them in a precise and interesting fashion:

1. They are spiritually negligent due to their own actions and prejudices; thus, they do not believe.
2. Their superstitious beliefs have entrapped them, and they are just like a camel, or another animal, that even if presented with water will not lower its head to drink. So too, such people refuse to metaphorically bow down and submit to the truth. In essence, they are enslaved from all sides.
3. In addition, there are veils over their eyes so they cannot look around and see the reality. Thus, these veils and barriers over their spiritual eyes are because of their own arrogant attitude towards Allah ﷻ and the realities around them – they were not imposed on them by the Almighty.

It is possible that the meaning of "The barrier in front of them" may refer to their long-term hopes and aspirations which they will never attain; while "The barrier behind them" may be a reference to their spiritual negligence that stems from their past misconduct which they never felt remorse or regret for and did not try to rectify. Thus, these two – their past wishes, and present neglect – are major obstacles in them being able to see the truth as it is; and they are two punishments which are placed in the way of such individuals as major forms of deviation.

Take Away Messages

1. There are countless lights *(Anwār)* which Allah ﷻ has made available for people to be guided by – such as the Quran, Prophet Muḥammad ﷺ, the Ahlul Bayt ﷺ, the

righteous saints *(Awliyā')*, and many more. However, some prefer to walk aimlessly, with blinders on their eyes. Eventually, they will fall and realize their wretched outcome.

2. The spiritually negligent unbelievers do not take lessons from the disbelievers who lived in the past and their outcomes. At the same time, they do not even take inspiration from the miracles and proofs which Allah ﷻ provides them that are right in front of them.

3. A disbeliever is one who is at a dead end in life and does not feel that they are able to progress. However, a believer realizes that there is never a dead end in life and that the doors towards Allah ﷻ are always open; and He is ever ready to accept anyone into His Mercy and Generosity.

4. In propagation of the teachings of Allah ﷻ, educating others about Monotheism *(Tawḥīd)*, and the other important tenants of religion, a person must provide logical proofs, and use analogies that will not only impact the intellect, but will also touch the emotions and feelings of other individuals.

Part 5: Warn Them or… – Verses 10-11

وَسَوَآءٌ عَلَيۡهِمۡ ءَأَنذَرۡتَهُمۡ أَمۡ لَمۡ تُنذِرۡهُمۡ لَا يُؤۡمِنُونَ ﴿١٠﴾ إِنَّمَا تُنذِرُ
مَنِ ٱتَّبَعَ ٱلذِّكۡرَ وَخَشِيَ ٱلرَّحۡمَٰنَ بِٱلۡغَيۡبِۖ فَبَشِّرۡهُ بِمَغۡفِرَةٖ وَأَجۡرٖ
كَرِيمٍ ﴿١١﴾

10. And it is all the same for them whether you warn them or you do not warn them, they will not believe (because they have deliberately shut their eyes and ears to the truth).

11. You can only warn those who will follow the Reminder (the Quran) and fear the All-Merciful (Allah ﷻ) in the unseen. Therefore, proclaim to them the glad tidings of forgiveness and a noble reward.

Thinking Points

The meaning of *'al-Dhikr'* or 'The Reminder' – keeping in mind how this word has been employed in other verses of the Noble Quran, is the **Quran itself**, as we see in verse 9 of Sūrah al-Ḥijr: "Surely, We have revealed the Reminder (the Quran), and We will surely be its guardian."[15]

Although all of humanity can potentially be guided to the Right Path, however, there are some disbelievers and polytheists who will **never** be guided [not because they

---

[15] Quran, Sūrah al-Ḥijr (15), Verse 9:

﴿إِنَّا نَحْنُ نَزَّلْنَا الذِّكْرَ وَإِنَّا لَهُ لَحَافِظُونَ﴾

cannot be guided – but rather, because they **do not** want to be guided]. Thus, the warnings of Prophet Muḥammad ﷺ to these sorts of individuals are ineffective – although as a part of the obligation to warn, the Prophet ﷺ would still convey the message to them.

We see that there are two groups of people who Allah ﷻ addresses as it relates to the guidance of His Message:

1. **The belligerent disbelievers *(kuffār):*** "Surely, those who disbelieve, it is all the same to them whether you warn them or you do not warn them, they will not believe."[16]
2. **The polytheists *(mushrikūn):*** "And if you invite them to guidance, they will not follow you; it is the same to you whether you invite them, or you are silent."[17]

Coming back to the verse under review, the meaning of the phrase '...and fear the Almighty in the unseen...' can potentially be one of the following:

1. The fear of Allah ﷻ which is deep inside an individual.
2. The awe of Allah ﷻ which a person feels when in seclusion and far from the prying eyes of other people.

---

[16] Quran, Sūrah al-Baqarah (2), Verse 6:

﴿إِنَّ الَّذِينَ كَفَرُوا سَوَاءٌ عَلَيْهِمْ أَأَنْذَرْتَهُمْ أَمْ لَمْ تُنْذِرْهُمْ لَا يُؤْمِنُونَ﴾

[17] Quran, Sūrah al-Aʿrāf (7), Verse 193:

﴿وَإِنْ تَدْعُوهُمْ إِلَى الْهُدَىٰ لَا يَتَّبِعُوكُمْ ۚ سَوَاءٌ عَلَيْكُمْ أَدَعَوْتُمُوهُمْ أَمْ أَنْتُمْ صَامِتُونَ﴾

3. The distress a person has with respect to the Court of Justice of Allah ﷻ on the Day of Resurrection, which is also one of the unseen realities.

When coming face to face with a great personality, the awe-inspiring and breath-taking persona of that individual can cause a person to "lose" oneself – and that state is referred to as 'reverential awe.' This human condition is something different than 'fear' or 'apprehension' which normally stems from realizing that there is a punishment or retribution awaiting an individual. Thus, 'reverential awe' is to humble oneself in the presence of someone due to their greatness [and this is what a true believer has in the presence of Allah ﷻ].

Take Away Messages

1. The benefits or outcomes which are derived from trying to advise an individual who has a spiritually constricted heart and is not willing to listen to or analyze what they are being told are the same as trying to drive an iron nail into a stone – it will be of no benefit.

2. The Completion of the Proof *(Itmām al-Ḥujjah)* is different from the potential influence which comes about through speaking and influencing people. In certain circumstances, people will not be affected by warnings and reminders; however, the Prophet ﷺ must still 'complete the argument' against these individuals and warn them – whether they accept it or not is up to them.

3. The Quran is a source of reminder, and reading and following its teachings will help the individual remember that which was learned in previous realms of existence but has since been forgotten. It also awakens the dormant natural human state *(fiṭrah)* which all of humanity were born with.

4. The expansive nature of the Divine Mercy of Allah ﷻ should not be a cause for our spiritual laziness. Of course, He is the All-Forgiving and All-Compassionate, however, we need to fulfil our role as His servants to the best of our ability [and keep away from sinning and not fulfilling our obligations].

5. A sign of true faith *(īmān)* and sincere reverential awe of Allah ﷻ *(taqwā)* is to be cautious of our actions even when we are in total seclusion and away from the eyes of people. We must realize that even though others do not see us, Allah ﷻ always observes what we are doing and what we are engaged in.

6. Fear *(khawf)* and hope *(rajā')* are two traits which a believer needs to have simultaneously and equally, and in the portion of the verse which reads 'they have the reverential awe of the All-Merciful in seclusion,' – both qualities are contained.

7. Having true consciousness of Allah ﷻ *(taqwā)* while in seclusion is especially important, and a believer must always have this trait. It is less than perfection in faith if a person shows this trait while in the public sphere but

disobeys Allah ﷻ in seclusion – leading to a double lifestyle.

8. The responsibility of the Prophets that Allah ﷻ sent to humanity was to warn people about the consequences of their actions, while at the same time keeping them optimistic and giving them hope.

9. An individual who pays heed to the warnings of the Prophets of Allah ﷻ is one who will receive the good tidings of Paradise.

Part 6: Total Accountability – Verse 12

إِنَّا نَحْنُ نُحْيِ ٱلْمَوْتَىٰ وَنَكْتُبُ مَا قَدَّمُوا۟ وَءَاثَـٰرَهُمْ ۚ وَكُلَّ شَىْءٍ
أَحْصَيْنَـٰهُ فِىٓ إِمَامٍ مُّبِينٍ ﴿١٢﴾

12. Surely, it is We alone Who raise the dead to life, and We shall preserve (their noble deeds) which they send forward and what they leave behind. And every (single) thing We have (comprehensively) preserved in a clear record.

Thinking Points

Everything which emanates by an individual is recorded in their record of deeds, and on the Day of Judgement it will be brought forth in the form of a book and given to each person.

Muslim scholars have noted that there are three types of such records:

1. **A personal book:** "And We had made known to the Banī Isrā'īl in the book."[18]
2. **A book for all the nations:** "And you will see every nation kneeling (from fear); every nation will be called to its book (and told): 'Today you shall be recompensed for what you did.'"[19]

---

[18] Quran, Sūrah al-Isrā' (17), Verse 4:

﴿وَقَضَيْنَا إِلَىٰ بَنِي إِسْرَائِيلَ فِي الْكِتَابِ﴾

[19] Quran, Sūrah al-Jāthiya (45), Verse 28:

3. **The comprehensive book:** "In a guarded tablet."[20]

It should be noted that the word *'imām'* or 'record' which is used for a book in the following verse: "And before it (was) the **book** *(imām)* of Mūsā, a guide, and a mercy"[21] can also be used for a leader, as in this verse: "Surely, I will make you a **leader** (an *imām*) for the people."[22] Although the word *imām* has multiple meanings, as seen, it can also refer to a book.

It has been mentioned in a *ḥadīth* that Imam ʿAlī ibn Abī Ṭālib ﷷ has also been referred to as an *'imām,'* and he is actually one of the manifestations of 'the manifest record' *(imām al-mubīn),* and as such, he possesses all forms of knowledge within himself – as given to him by Prophet Muḥammad ﷺ through the explicit permission of Allah ﷻ.[23]

Most of the commentators of the Quran state that the meaning of 'the manifest record' is 'the protected tablet'

﴿وَتَرَىٰ كُلَّ أُمَّةٍ جَاثِيَةً ۚ كُلُّ أُمَّةٍ تُدْعَىٰ إِلَىٰ كِتَابِهَا الْيَوْمَ تُجْزَوْنَ مَا كُنتُمْ تَعْمَلُونَ﴾

[20] Quran, Sūrah al-Burūj (85), Verse 22:

﴿فِي لَوْحٍ مَّحْفُوظٍ﴾

[21] Quran, Sūrah Hūd (11), Verse 17:

﴿وَمِن قَبْلِهِ كِتَابُ مُوسَىٰ إِمَامًا وَرَحْمَةً﴾

[22] Quran, Sūrah al-Baqarah (2), Verse 124:

﴿قَالَ إِنِّي جَاعِلُكَ لِلنَّاسِ إِمَامًا﴾

[23] Ḥuwayzī, ʿAbd ʿAlī ibn Jumuʿa al-, *Tafsīr Nūr al-Thaqalayn.*

which has been referred to in the Quran as being 'The Origin (or Mother of the) Book.'[24] Seeing as how this Book sent by Allah ﷻ contains all types of knowledge, and everything is contained within it, and everyone is compelled to enact its contents, thus it is referred to as a 'manifest Book.'[25]

Take Away Messages

1. A person must speak clearly and unequivocally about the distorted and diversionary beliefs of the unbelievers. When it comes to calling out such things, we cannot be diplomatic or cover up the issues.
2. As every human being is bound to die eventually, we must realize that we will all be brought back to life on the Day of Resurrection to be held to account for our actions in this life.
3. The record of everything which a person did in one's life, as well as the actions that took place after one's death – both the good deeds that others sent on behalf of the deceased, or acts of goodness which carried on after one's death, such as knowledge they left behind, water wells they provided for others, and all other acts of perpetual goodness; as well as sins that they introduced into society and people continue to perform – all of these will be

[24] Quran, Sūrah al-Zukhruf (43), Verse 4:

﴿وَإِنَّهُۥ فِىٓ أُمِّ ٱلْكِتَـٰبِ لَدَيْنَا لَعَلِىٌّ حَكِيمٌ ۝٤﴾

[25] Rafsanjānī, ʿAlī Akbar Hāshemī, *Tafsīr Rāhnumā.*

preserved, and the record of these actions will be opened on the Day of Judgement.

4. It is not only a person's actions and words, rather even all the effects of what they do are being recorded and will be included in the accounting on the Day of Recompense. This includes virtuous deeds and their residual remains, such as the endowments given, perpetual charity which continue to benefit others, knowledge which they taught to people that sustained, etc. At the same time, all of one's bad deeds and their remnants will also be presented, such as if one established venue of sins and debauchery – they will also carry the burden of the by-products of those actions.

5. On the Day of Judgement, people will only be preoccupied with Allah ﷻ and their own situation, no one will have time to worry about others.

6. Human beings are not only responsible for their own actions, but they will also be responsible for the long-ranging consequences of their deeds which remain and continue long after their passing.

7. In determining our rewards and retributions, the calculating apparatus of Allah ﷻ is extremely accurate.

8. In the Divine Court of Allah ﷻ on the Day of Judgement, the accounts of every person will be taken very precisely, and they will be clear and well-defined.

Part 7: A True Story – Verse 13

وَٱضْرِبْ لَهُم مَّثَلًا أَصْحَـٰبَ ٱلْقَرْيَةِ إِذْ جَآءَهَا ٱلْمُرْسَلُونَ ﴿١٣﴾

13. And present to them an example: the people of the city when the Messengers (of Allah) came to it.

Thinking Points

From verse 13 and continuing for another seventeen verses, the Quran begins to narrate the story of several Prophets sent directly by Allah ﷻ for the guidance of a specific group of people. As we will see, these individuals were responsible for guiding the people of their own geographic region to the teachings of Allah ﷻ – namely, Monotheism *(Tawḥīd)*.

It has been mentioned in the Books of *Tafsīr* of the Quran that the city or town spoken about in this verse is some portion of the region of present-day Antakya. This was an ancient town in the old part of the Roman Empire and today is a part of the Republic of Türkiye[26] which was a bustling city of commerce and trade.

By reading and studying these eighteen verses, we can conclude that the people of this town were idol-worshippers, and it is for this reason that Allah ﷻ sent a series of Prophets to them to guide them to the path of Monotheism *(Tawḥīd)* and fight against polytheism *(shirk)*.

[26] Previously known as the country of Turkey. (Tr.)

Take Away Messages

1. Studying the history of those who lived in the past is the best lesson for those living in the present.

2. An educator and religious propagator must be aware of the history of the past for many reasons – one of them being that they can derive lessons for how they should act in their era.

3. There are firm principles and rules which govern societies, and the destiny of humanity and societies can be determined based on these principles. The Divine Traditions *(Sunnatullāh)* are immutable, and do not differ when it comes to various nations, individuals, times, or places – just as universal laws such as gravity apply in all times and places.

4. The best examples which we should employ when speaking with others are those that are real and objective – not imaginative.

5. When it comes to relating a story, the **lessons to be learned** are important – the incidental aspects of the story such as the name of the region, the names of the individuals involved, the language spoken, or the number of individuals, etc., are immaterial and usually irrelevant. They may be nice to know, however, they do not impact the lesson which is being taught.

6. The Prophets sent by Allah ﷻ went in search of people to guide them – they did not wait for people to come to them looking for guidance.

Part 8: The Three Messengers – Verses 14-17

إِذْ أَرْسَلْنَآ إِلَيْهِمُ ٱثْنَيْنِ فَكَذَّبُوهُمَا فَعَزَّزْنَا بِثَالِثٍ فَقَالُوٓا۟ إِنَّآ إِلَيْكُم
مُّرْسَلُونَ ﴿١٤﴾ قَالُوا۟ مَآ أَنتُمْ إِلَّا بَشَرٌ مِّثْلُنَا وَمَآ أَنزَلَ ٱلرَّحْمَٰنُ مِن
شَىْءٍ إِنْ أَنتُمْ إِلَّا تَكْذِبُونَ ﴿١٥﴾ قَالُوا۟ رَبُّنَا يَعْلَمُ إِنَّآ إِلَيْكُمْ
لَمُرْسَلُونَ ﴿١٦﴾ وَمَا عَلَيْنَآ إِلَّا ٱلْبَلَٰغُ ٱلْمُبِينُ ﴿١٧﴾

14. (At first) We sent two (messengers), but they (the people of that town) rejected both (of them), then We strengthened them (the two messengers) with a third, so they said: 'Indeed, we are messengers (sent) to you (by Allah ﷻ).'

15. They (the rejecters of those two messengers) gave (a general) reply: 'You are only human beings like us, and the All-Merciful (Allah ﷻ) has not revealed a thing (to you). You are simply telling lies.'

16. They said: 'Our Lord knows that we are indeed messengers sent to you,

17. And our duty is only to convey (the message) in clear terms.'

Thinking Points

There are some who believe in Allah ﷻ, however, they do not accept Prophethood, nor revelation. They do not believe that

Allah ﷻ sent certain chosen individuals to humanity with revelations, and to be practical guides and role models. These types of people say that Allah ﷻ has given everyone an intellect, so there is no need for Divine revelation.

This sort of belief stems from an incorrect understanding of Allah ﷻ – just as we see in another verse of the Quran which states: "And they do not appraise Allah with true appraisal when they say: 'Allah did not reveal anything to a mortal.'"[27]

Take Away Messages

1. Sometimes, inviting the truth, encouraging the good and forbidding evil must be done collectively, rather than individually. As individuals, our ability to effectively bring about change in society may be limited; however, if we work together, there is a greater chance that we will be able to bring about positive changes in an individual or society.
2. Stubbornness and inflexibility are sicknesses which cannot be cured with ease and sometimes cannot be cured at all. As such, we see that sometimes even the Prophets which Allah ﷻ sent for the guidance and betterment of humanity were outright rejected.

---

[27] Quran, Sūrah al-Anʿām (6), Verse 91:

﴿وَمَا قَدَرُوا اللَّهَ حَقَّ قَدْرِهِ إِذْ قَالُوا مَا أَنْزَلَ اللَّهُ عَلَىٰ بَشَرٍ مِنْ شَيْءٍ﴾

3. Do not simply give up on your task or mission by discarding and rebuffing your opponents and thinking that they will never change. Rather, strengthen yourself by bringing others on board to assist you in your work.

4. Sometimes, multiple Prophets were sent by Allah ﷻ at one time to a specific region for the guidance of a community.

5. The number of people involved in propagation should be proportionate to the needs of the society that they are going to be dealing with. It is illogical to think that one *muballigh* – propagator/educator – can impact a community of hundreds or thousands of people.

6. When it comes to principles of management and administration, when you appoint an individual and give them certain responsibilities to fulfill, then do not impede them in any way and never micro-manage them. Rather, ensure that you support them in whatever way you can, and give them the tools to be successful.

7. Having many people who are fit to carry out a certain task will lead to the respect and admiration of all of them in society. Generally, when two or more people are working together and have similar goals and objectives, and others see them as clicking together and as individuals who support one another, they will be equally respected, and society will appreciate how they can function together with no sense of competition between each other.

8. The praise and credit that some people are showered with, as well as the humiliation that other people may face in the life of this world are both determined by Allah ﷻ; although sometimes there is an intermediary involved that could either shower the praise or abase individuals. However, ultimately, Allah ﷻ is the One who ensures that those who are worthy of praise in society are awarded it, and those who merit dishonour are also given it.
9. When it comes to principles of management, we must always have some backup support plan in place just in case things fall through.
10. The belligerent disbelievers always ignore perfections around them, and usually only look at things with the physical eyes, rather than the metaphysical realities present.
11. There are some people who feel that religious responsibilities such as the requirement to perform certain actions and refrain from acts which are prohibited in the faith, as well as encouraging others towards good and forbidding evil are against the Mercy of Allah ﷻ. Such people presume that the meaning of the Mercy of Allah ﷻ is that there must be limitless freedoms in society, and that people should be able to do whatever they wish as only He can judge them, and He can forgive His servants. However, this is completely incorrect! In fact, the Mercy of Allah ﷻ necessitates that guidelines and restrictions must be in place for everyone to follow.

In short, laws and regulations are a mercy, while chaos and anarchy are demonic.

12. In response to the unremitting denials of adversaries, a person must work hard to calm their own soul through the constant remembrance of Allah ﷻ.

13. The responsibility of the Prophets sent by Allah ﷻ was to make the path clear, and plainly articulate what they were to convey, however, they were not responsible for the outcome which would result from their efforts.

Part 9: The Belief in Superstitions – Verses 18-19

> قَالُوٓاْ إِنَّا تَطَيَّرۡنَا بِكُمۡۖ لَئِن لَّمۡ تَنتَهُواْ لَنَرۡجُمَنَّكُمۡ وَلَيَمَسَّنَّكُم مِّنَّا
> عَذَابٌ أَلِيمٞ ١٨ قَالُواْ طَٰٓئِرُكُم مَّعَكُمۡۚ أَئِن ذُكِّرۡتُمۚ بَلۡ أَنتُمۡ قَوۡمٞ
> مُّسۡرِفُونَ ١٩
>
> 18. They (the people of the town) said: 'Indeed, we consider you a bad omen (for we are seized with one calamity or another after your arrival). If you do not desist (give up your preaching), then we will certainly stone you, and a painful punishment shall befall you at our hands.'
>
> 19. They (the Prophets sent to the people of the town) said: Your omen (ill fate) is your own making. (Do you say all of this) because you have been admonished? Rather, you are transgressing people.'

Thinking Points

Belief in bad omens is not merely a superstitious creed that existed only in the past, but it is also something that is seen around the world today – in the "East," as well as in the "West," and each group have their own things which they consider as being 'bad luck.'[28]

---

[28] Many countries in the so-called West consider some of the strangest of things as being bad omens, such as walking under a

Islam considers belief in such superstitions as being nothing more than a shade of polytheism, and by using the phrase: 'The belief in bad omens is (a form of) polytheism,'[29] it has sought to cancel all such thoughts. The penitence *(kaffārah)* for having belief in such things is to put full trust and reliance *(tawakkul)* in Allah ﷻ, as the saying goes: "The penitence for having belief in bad luck is to have full trust and reliance in Allah."[30]

Believing in bad omens has a negative impact on an individual and can lead a person to evil deeds such as having bad thoughts about others, obstructing one's daily functions of life, leading one towards failure, and feelings of humiliation. Even worse than all of this is when people feel that the sacred symbols of faith, or the friends of Allah ﷻ *(Awliyāʾ)*, are bad omens for them.

---

ladder; having a 13th floor in a building; having a black cat cross your path, and many other such fables. Muslims need to ensure that they reject such superstitions, and things that come from their own personal culture which have nothing at all to do with Islam.

[29] ʿAllāmah Majlisī, *Biḥār al-Anwār*, Vol. 55, Pg. 322. The Arabic text of this tradition is as follows:

أَلطِّيَرَةُ شِرْكٌ.

[30] Shaykh Kulaynī, *Al-Kāfī*, Vol. 8, Pg. 198. The Arabic text of this tradition is as follows:

كَفَّارَةُ الطِّيَرَةِ التَّوَكُّلُ.

Take Away Messages

1. There must be clear answers to any forms of deviations present in society.
2. Denial, humiliation, and threats are weapons which belligerent disbelievers often use against righteous individuals.
3. Asking other people to perform any action which they claim will allow them to see into the future, as well as any form of fortune telling is from the habits of the Period of Ignorance *(Jāhiliyyah)* before the advent of Islam, and are impermissible to engage in.
4. Those who lack real intellect will resort to superstitious beliefs and practices.
5. Oftentimes, mental deviations of an individual result in practical deviations of society.
6. Disbelief can lead a person to hardness of the spiritual heart and even enable them to have the audacity to threaten the Prophets sent by Allah ﷻ.
7. The belligerent disbelievers are individuals who, in the face of the logical and clear proofs of the Prophets sent by Allah ﷻ, had no logical foundation of their own, thus once they belied something, they then resorted to threatening the individuals who brought the proofs.
8. The role of Prophets sent by Allah ﷻ was to awaken the spiritually heedless individuals and get them to focus on the sound innate human nature *(fiṭrah)*.

9. One of the manifestations of extravagance *(isrāf)* is to cause agitation in society.

10. The root of misery in life is insurgency against Allah ﷻ, and extravagance against the Prophets sent by Allah ﷻ and their messages, as well as not believing in Allah ﷻ and His Divinely-sent Prophets.

Part 10: Assisting those on the Path – Verses 20-21

وَجَآءَ مِنۡ أَقۡصَا ٱلۡمَدِينَةِ رَجُلٞ يَسۡعَىٰ قَالَ يَٰقَوۡمِ ٱتَّبِعُواْ ٱلۡمُرۡسَلِينَ ٢٠

ٱتَّبِعُواْ مَن لَّا يَسۡـَٔلُكُمۡ أَجۡرٗا وَهُم مُّهۡتَدُونَ ٢١

20. And there came a man running from the farthest end of the town. He said: 'O my people, follow the Messengers!

21. Follow those who do not ask you for any payment (reward), and they are (rightly) guided.'

A *Mujāhid* Ready to Give His Life

In the verses under review, we see another aspect of the struggles that the three Messengers who were previously mentioned had to go through, and it is related to the planned, courageous support of the few believers around them. These few people stood up against the unbelieving, polytheistic, stubborn majority, and defended the Messengers sent by Allah ﷻ right to the very end – ready to even give up their own lives to support the cause.

The event begins by Allah ﷻ telling us about a man of faith who came running from a distant part of the city towards a group of disbelievers, saying to his people that they must believe in the Messengers that Allah ﷻ sent to them.

Most commentators of the Quran have noted that the name of this man who came running was Ḥabīb al-Najjār,[31] and that he was one of those who, in his first encounters with the Messengers sent by Allah ﷻ, realized the depth of their teachings and the truth of their call, and became a steadfast and determined believer in them.

When news reached him that in the heart of the city, the people had revolted against these Divinely-sent Prophets and there was a possibility that the people were planning to kill them, he realized that silence was not an option.

In this regard, the Quran uses the word *'yasʿa,'* which is translated as 'running.' In other words, the Quran makes it explicitly clear that this man did not walk, but rather, he ran to reach the city centre to see the situation with his own eyes, and do whatever he could to support and defend the Messengers sent by Allah ﷻ despite the odds being stacked against him.

When speaking about this individual, whom we noted was most likely Ḥabīb al-Najjār, the Quran uses the indefinite noun, 'a man' *(rajul).* This may be done to show those who read this story in the Quran that Ḥabīb was just an "ordinary person." He did not possess extraordinary strength, or power, or many followers to support him – he was alone in this goal to assist in the propagation of the Word of Allah ﷻ.

Even though he was a minority in believing in the Messengers sent by Allah ﷻ, the light and passion of true

---

[31] He is also known as the 'True Believer of Āle Yāsīn' *(Muʾmin Āle Yāsīn)* and 'The Individual Mentioned in Yāsīn' *(Ṣāḥib Āle Yāsīn)*, however, he is best known by his name, Ḥabīb al-Najjār.

faith *(īmān)* illuminated him such that he ignored the consequences of what may happen to him, and entered the battlefield of devotion, ready to defend the teachings of Monotheism *(Tawḥīd).*

By him remaining unknown in this story, through both the use of the indefinite noun, as well as his name not being mentioned in the Quran, it was perhaps a wakeup call by Allah ﷻ to the believers in the era of Prophet Muḥammad ﷺ – and especially at the beginning of the message of Islam in Mecca – that even if believers are few, they could take this unknown person as their role model.

Through reading this beautiful story preserved in Sūrah Yāsīn, the people would realize that even if a believer is alone, they still have the responsibility to stand up for the truth and that silence is never an option.

Another interesting term which the Quran uses in this passage is '*aqṣāl Madīna*' translated as 'the furthest part of the city.' This phrase conveys to the reader that the invitation of these Messengers extended to the remote parts of the city, and it had influenced the hearts of many individuals – not just those who lived in the city centre.

Historically, and to an extent, even what can be seen today in traditional communities and societies, the remote parts of a city are where the marginalized people reside. Most often than not, as their minds are not preoccupied by the busy life of big cities, they are more prepared to accept the Message of Truth when it comes to them. On the contrary, well-to-do people tend to live in the heart of the city, and it is harder to attract them to the truth as they are usually caught up in the pursuit of temporal pleasures, oblivious to issues of spirituality.

The third interesting term which Allah ﷻ uses in this discussion is the phrase '*yā qawm,*' translated as 'O my people.'

This beautiful expression demonstrates the compassion of this man, Ḥabīb al-Najjār, towards the people of the city. It also shows the sincerity with which he extended the invitation to follow the Messengers, and that he had no ulterior motives or personal gain from the message he was endorsing.

So, what logic did Ḥabīb, this brave, dedicated, and sincere individual who was struggling in the Way of Allah ﷻ *(mujāhid),* use to attract the attention of his fellow citizens?

First, he said: "Follow those who do not ask you for a reward for their mission."

This is the first sign of a person's sincerity – they do not stand to gain any material benefit in their calling, and do not ask for money, position in society, thanks, gratitude, or any other reward for their services.

This concept is seen many times in the Quran when Allah ﷻ speaks about the great Prophets He sent for the guidance of humanity. In a clear display of their sincerity, impartiality, and purity of their hearts, they proclaim how they want nothing from those who listen to their message.

For example, in Sūrah al-Shuʿarāʾ, this theme comes five times where Allah ﷻ quotes His Prophets as saying: "And we ask you no reward. Our reward is only with the Lord of all the Worlds."[32]

Coming back to Sūrah Yāsīn, Ḥabīb then went on to say: "In addition, these Messengers, as can be seen from the content of their invitations and words, are people who are themselves guided *(muhtadūn).*"

He wanted to point out the fact that refusing to accept someone's invitation is either because:

1. The invitation is not right and leads to misguidance.
2. The invitation is right, but those who propose it will benefit from others following them.

This is a cause of skepticism about such an invitation; however, when there are neither of these at play, as it relates to the Prophets that Allah ﷻ sent, then how can there be any shred of doubt in their invitation?![33]

Take Away Messages

1. Living far away from the city does not necessarily mean that one is far away from the culture of that place, or that such a person cannot relate to the people there.

2. Supporting the truth has no limits or boundaries.

---

[32] Quran, Sūrah al-Shuʿarā' (26), Verses 109, 127, 145, 164, and 180:

﴿وَمَآ أَسْـَٔلُكُمْ عَلَيْهِ مِنْ أَجْرٍ إِنْ أَجْرِىَ إِلَّا عَلَىٰ رَبِّ ٱلْعَـٰلَمِينَ ١٠٩﴾

[33] As *Tafsīr-e Nūr* had no commentary on this passage, we extracted and translated this portion from *Tafsīr-e Nemunah.*

3. Sometimes it takes just one person to make a move and make a call for help for others to hear and respond. In this regard, Imam ʿAlī ibn Abī Ṭālib ﷺ has been quoted as saying: "Never feel afraid due to the few numbers of people on the right path."[34]

4. To assist on the path of the truth, one should never consider the lengthy physical distances that one may need to travel as being an impediment – even if one needs to trek long distances to find the true teachings, they need to do so.

5. Standing on the side of the truth requires an individual to have the right motivation and a burning desire to bring about a change in themselves – not merely a title or label associated with them.

6. Supporting the truth must be accompanied by multiple feelings and sentiments such as a burning desire to act and effect change, the love to exert effort, the ability to use logic, and the feeling of affection for others.

7. Breaking the silence by speaking aloud and clear in the face of deviations and assisting the leaders who are on the path of the truth are all acts highly praised by Allah ﷻ.

8. Having sincerity in the propagation of faith is one of the conditions required to attract people; therefore, those

---

[34] *Nahj al-Balāgha*, Sermon 201. The Arabic text of this tradition is as follows:

أَيُّهَا النَّاسُ، لَا تَسْتَوْحِشُوا فِي طَرِيقِ الْهُدَىٰ لِقِلَّةِ أَهْلِهِ.

who are calling others to the truth should not expect that people will compensate them financially for their guidance.[35]

9. Those who wish to guide people to the truth must first be guided to be able to influence others.

[35] Those who work to educate and propagate the faith do not demand financial compensation for their work, as they believe that their rewards in this world and the next are solely with Allah ﷻ; however, they still need to live, pay their bills, take care of their families, etc. Thus, although they may not stipulate a price in return for their efforts, those who benefit from them or ask for their guidance should realize that they must provide an appropriate amount of remuneration for the time and energies which they expend in the way of propagation of the Message of Allah ﷻ. (Tr.)

Part 11: Reward for the Steadfast – Verses 22-27

وَمَا لِىَ لَآ أَعۡبُدُ ٱلَّذِى فَطَرَنِى وَإِلَيۡهِ تُرۡجَعُونَ ﴿٢٢﴾ ءَأَتَّخِذُ مِن دُونِهِۦٓ
ءَالِهَةً إِن يُرِدۡنِ ٱلرَّحۡمَٰنُ بِضُرࣲّ لَّا تُغۡنِ عَنِّى شَفَٰعَتُهُمۡ شَيۡـࣰٔا وَلَا
يُنقِذُونِ ﴿٢٣﴾ إِنِّىٓ إِذࣰا لَّفِى ضَلَٰلࣲ مُّبِينٍ ﴿٢٤﴾ إِنِّىٓ ءَامَنتُ
بِرَبِّكُمۡ فَٱسۡمَعُونِ ﴿٢٥﴾ قِيلَ ٱدۡخُلِ ٱلۡجَنَّةَۖ قَالَ يَٰلَيۡتَ قَوۡمِى يَعۡلَمُونَ
﴿٢٦﴾ بِمَا غَفَرَ لِى رَبِّى وَجَعَلَنِى مِنَ ٱلۡمُكۡرَمِينَ ﴿٢٧﴾

22. 'And why should I not worship Him Who created me, and to Whom you (all) will be brought back?

23. Shall I take other than Him (false) deities (while), if the All-Merciful intends for me some harm, their intercession will be of no avail to me, nor can they save me (from any adversity)?

24. Surely, I would then be in manifest error.

25. Surely, I have believed in your (true) Lord, therefore listen to me.'

26. It was said (to him by Allah ﷻ): 'Enter Paradise.' He said: 'O, I wish my people could know,

27. Of how my Lord has forgiven me and placed me among the honoured ones.'

Thinking Points

According to what is mentioned in *Tafsīr Majmaʿ al-Bayān*, this story in Sūrah Yāsīn is regarding an event which transpired during the era of Prophet ʿIsā ﷺ in which two of his disciples *(ḥawāriyūn)* were sent to Antakya[36] to invite the people to believe in the One True God.

On the way there, they met up with a person named Ḥabīb al-Najjār, and after those two disciples of Prophet ʿIsā ﷺ performed a miracle, Ḥabīb ended up accepting the religion they were propagating.

The two disciples of Prophet ʿIsā ﷺ entered the city, however, the residents rejected their message and began to oppose them. Prophet ʿIsā ﷺ then sent Shimʿūn, one of the senior-most disciples, to help and support the two previous believers which had been sent. Through earning the trust of the King of that region, Shimʿūn was able to bring him and most of the people of that town to the true teachings of Monotheism, leaving their previous belief system.

As good as it sounds, and noting that this narration has also been mentioned in other books of *tafsīr* of the Quran, however, for the following reasons, this story does not fit with the text of the Quranic narrative:

1. From the apparent reading of the verses in this chapter, it was Allah ﷻ who sent the Prophets to this town – not that it was a Prophet who sent his disciples.

[36] The modern form of Antioch is a municipality and the capital district of Hatay Province, Türkiye. (Tr.)

2. If most of the people accepted the message, then there should not have been a punishment sent down to them.[37]

Therefore, according to the more authentic narrations, the individual sent to support the Messengers deputed by Allah ﷻ to the city of Antakya was Ḥabīb al-Najjār, who is also commonly known as *Ṣāḥib Yāsīn* – the person of (Sūrah) Yāsīn. We believe that he was at the same spiritual level as the believer among the followers of the Pharaoh *(Mu'min Āle Fir'awn)* who rose up to help and support Prophet Mūsā ﷺ against the Pharaoh.[38]

Today, the city of Antakya lies between the two cities of Ḥalab and Iskandariyya and is a part of Türkiye; and after Jerusalem *(Bayt al-Muqaddas)*, from the historical perspective, it was considered the second most important city for Christians.

Take Away Messages

1. Those who refuse to submit to the Creator will be condemned in the court of their own consciousness well before being condemned in the Court of Allah ﷻ on the Day of Judgement.

2. One of the ways to invite others to the path of Allah ﷻ is to logically explain to them their own conviction and belief system.

---

[37] *Tafsīr-e Nemunah.*

[38] *Tafsīr Majma' al-Bayān; Tafsīr Nūr al-Thaqalayn.*

3. Focusing on the source of our existence and our eventual outcome that we came from Allah ﷻ and will return to Allah ﷻ can help to cement the root of true submission to the Almighty.

4. One of the ways to teach others is through drawing comparisons. Allah ﷻ is the One Who created us, while the worthless idols that some choose to follow bring about absolutely no benefit to humanity.

5. The different challenges which people face are all through the Will and Intention of Allah ﷻ, and pivot around His Mercy.

6. For a person to be able to focus better on Allah ﷻ, they should imagine themselves being put face to face with extreme challenges in life and then think of how they will get out of them.

7. In order not to play with the emotions and sentiments of people and hurt their feelings, we should always use ourselves as examples when speaking to others.

8. The best way to invite others to Allah ﷻ is through our own practical actions.

9. Martyrdom in the way of supporting the Divinely-sent leaders, and in the path of encouraging good has a long history to it and is the way of the people sent by Allah ﷻ for the guidance of humanity.

10. There is no gap between attaining martyrdom and entering Paradise.

11. Even after martyrdom, the devotees of Allah ﷻ are still concerned about those who are alive.

12. The intermediary life and paradise in the grave (*barzakhī* state) come before the perpetual Paradise in the final abode.

13. Martyrdom is one of the ways in which a person can be pardoned for their past sins.

Part 12: Definite Punishment of Allah – Verses 28-29

وَمَآ أَنزَلْنَا عَلَىٰ قَوْمِهِۦ مِنۢ بَعْدِهِۦ مِن جُندٍ مِّنَ ٱلسَّمَآءِ وَمَا كُنَّا
مُنزِلِينَ ﴿٢٨﴾ إِن كَانَتْ إِلَّا صَيْحَةً وَٰحِدَةً فَإِذَا هُمْ خَٰمِدُونَ ﴿٢٩﴾

28. And We did not send down upon his people after him any soldiers from heaven (to destroy them), nor would We have ever done so.

29. It was not but a single blast, and immediately they were all extinguished.

Thinking Points

In the previous verses, the outcome of an individual, whom the *ḥadīth* refer to as Ḥabīb al-Najjār, was discussed. He was that sole individual who stood up in support of the Prophets sent by Allah ﷻ, and called others to assist him and the message of the men deputed by the Almighty. However, as we saw in the previous sections, he was martyred for his unwavering commitment to the message of truth.

The verses under review speak about the downfall of the obstinate disbelievers who belied the Messengers sent by Allah ﷻ, and even ended up killing Ḥabīb.

Reviewing the verses in this section, the word '*khāmid*' which is used at the end of verse 29 comes from the ʿArabic word '*khumūd*' which usually means 'to put out the hot coals of a fire,' but here in the verse under review, it means 'utter destruction and death.'

Take Away Messages

1. Angels are the agents of Allah ﷻ, and they bring either Divine Mercy or inflict Divine fury upon the people depending on the orders of the Almighty. All their actions are performed by the decree of Allah ﷻ and they are in no position to do anything on their own accord.
2. Although Allah ﷻ sends warnings and signs when a community is going down the wrong path, at the end of the day, His wrath is sudden which we must never overlook or become heedless about.
3. Sometimes, the people of an entire region are destroyed due to them shedding the blood of one innocent believer. Allah ﷻ does not necessarily engage in collective punishment, however, when an act of aggression takes place and others in society see what is going on and remain silent and indifferent, providing their tacit approval for what transpired, they are all equally guilty of the crime.
4. The Quran shows us that the superpowers who had initially said: "We will stone you, or make you face a terrible, painful punishment," were easily destroyed by Allah ﷻ with one swipe.

Part 13: Rejection of the Emissaries – Verse 30

يَٰحَسۡرَةً عَلَى ٱلۡعِبَادِۚ مَا يَأۡتِيهِم مِّن رَّسُولٍ إِلَّا كَانُواْ بِهِۦ
يَسۡتَهۡزِءُونَ ٣٠

30. Alas, how regretful for the servants! Not a single Messenger came to (reform) them, but they ridiculed him.

Thinking Points

In this verse which rounds up the discussion of the story of the Messengers sent by Allah ﷻ, as well as the inclusion of the individual who the *ḥadīth* refer to as Ḥabīb al-Najjār, the Quran uses a unique and effective tone in conveying the message of the Almighty.

Allah ﷻ makes a general note of all the renegades throughout history, and how they reacted to the invitation of the Messengers which Allah ﷻ sent to humanity. Although they have different names throughout the ages, history has shown that tyrants and despots resort to one standard tactic – ridiculing and mocking the Messengers and their message. This can be seen from the time when the first Prophet of Allah ﷻ was deputed to humanity with a Divinely crafted mission, and continued until the last of His emissaries, Prophet Muḥammad ﷺ.

How sad that a person can recognize the truth and still decide to close the doors of the Mercy of Allah ﷻ towards oneself! Shame on such people who try to extinguish the lights of guidance from Allah ﷻ.

Utterly spiritually and morally bankrupt, and deprived of any type of prosperity, such individuals do not heed the call of the leaders that Allah ﷻ sends. Rather, they go a step further and mock them, and then even threaten to kill them – and sometimes, they carry out their assassination plots. Such people go through with their nefarious plans even though they have seen the outcome of the rebels who disbelieved in God who came before them. They hear the stories of those who transgressed in the past; or they read the anecdotes of those who tried to shut down the Message of Allah ﷻ; however, they refuse to learn a lesson from this and end up walking the same path – ultimately ending up in the same fate as those who came before them.

A point to keep in mind in this portion of Sūrah Yāsīn, as well as can be seen in other parts of the Noble Quran, is that although we know the entire Quran is from Allah ﷻ and are His Words, however, the verse under review is considered as the "direct speech" and "sentiment" of Allah ﷻ within this story.

The word *'ḥasrata'* has been translated as 'how regretful' and it refers to a deep, inner sense of remorse and guilt which comes about from past events that were out of a person's control. Such emotions can never be attributed to Allah ﷻ as He does not have states like remorse, anger, rage, etc. Thus, the way we can understand this verse is that although, as we said, it is the speech of Allah ﷻ, however, the state of these dark days was such that every person was aware of the situation, felt sorry, and was deeply affected. They said to themselves: "Why is it that even with all of these means of rescue which Allah ﷻ sent for humanity, these people have decided to allow themselves to drown in this terrible whirlpool of loss?"

Lastly, the fact that Allah ﷻ uses the term *'ʿibād'* – or 'the servants' (of Allah ﷻ) – refers to the reality that there is an aura of surprise being explained in the Quran in which it is startling that despite being overwhelmed by His blessings, still there are some servants of Allah ﷻ who resort to the committing of such crimes against themselves and others.

Take Away Messages

1. A believer who places oneself alongside the truth is in the best position to call others towards it, and by following the Prophets which Allah ﷻ sent, they will become successful. Thus, such a person will never act with obstinacy, or place oneself in the way of Divine punishment.
2. Stubbornness will lead a person to ignore spiritual growth; and neglecting the path of proximity to Allah ﷻ will be the start of a life of regret.
3. Being aware of the bitter events of the past will ensure that a person will not repeat making those same mistakes in one's own life.
4. Mocking the Prophets that Allah ﷻ sent is something which the disbelievers have done throughout history.

5. All the Prophets that Allah ﷻ sent have been mocked and ridiculed in their lives in some way or another. Therefore, those who are working to propagate the religion should also anticipate that they will face verbal assaults and/or insults from others.

Part 14: Ruin of Past Generations – Verses 31-32

أَلَمْ يَرَوْا۟ كَمْ أَهْلَكْنَا قَبْلَهُم مِّنَ ٱلْقُرُونِ أَنَّهُمْ إِلَيْهِمْ لَا يَرْجِعُونَ ﴿٣١﴾ وَإِن كُلٌّ لَّمَّا جَمِيعٌ لَّدَيْنَا مُحْضَرُونَ ﴿٣٢﴾

31. Have they not seen how many generations We destroyed before them, and that those (generations) will never come back to them (after their destruction)?

32. And indeed, all of them will most certainly be brought (back) before Us.

Thinking Points

The word '*qarn*' which is the singular form of '*qurūn*' means 'generation,' and according to what has been mentioned in *Tafsīr-e Nemunah,* it is a word which is applicable to both 'a long period of time' and for 'people who live during a particular era.'

Take Away Messages

1. Those who do not research history, or do not take a lesson from the outcome of the people of the past are admonished in the Quran.
2. The Tradition of Allah ﷻ *(Sunnatullāh)* that are seen in history are unchanging. Thus, if something transpires in

history, we must realize that it is not a one-off thing – it is bound to happen again. Therefore, whatever we learn from past events can be used when we analyze other occurrences which transpire – even in present times.

3. Recounting historical events and ensuring that others are aware of them is an ideal way to warn people before they end up performing the same actions, having to suffer the same fate as those in the past. It also gives solace to those who are traversing the right path in life that even if they are wronged, there will be repercussions for the guilty.

4. The outcome of ridiculing the Prophets which Allah ﷻ sent will be the obliteration of those who participate in such crimes.

5. After the Divine wrath has been manifested, there will be no way to return and make amends for one's evil ways, thus we must never miss opportunities to improve and change our fate.

6. The annihilation of the belligerent disbelievers is not their end – it may be the end of their life in this temporal world; however, it is merely the beginning of their eventual torment which will happen in the grave and the world to come.

7. All of humanity will be raised up in one place on the Day of Resurrection to be held accountable for their actions.

Part 15: Sign of Allah – Reviving the Earth – Verse 33

وَءَايَةٌ لَّهُمُ ٱلْأَرْضُ ٱلْمَيْتَةُ أَحْيَيْنَـٰهَا وَأَخْرَجْنَا مِنْهَا حَبًّا فَمِنْهُ يَأْكُلُونَ ﴿٣٣﴾

33. And a sign for them is the dead earth which We bring to life, and from which We bring forth (a large variety of) grains what they eat.

Thinking Points

In the previous verse, we read that all of humanity will be brought back to life on the Day of Resurrection and will be standing in the presence of Allah ﷻ.

The verse under review offers an example of how the dead earth is brought back to life, and Allah ﷻ presents this example as a parallel for the confirmation of the physical Day of Resurrection of humanity, and how everyone will be brought back to life on that Day according to the Will of Allah ﷻ.

Take Away Messages

1. Every seed and plant which grows from the earth can be thought of as a person who did not exist. They are brought into this world, given life, will die, then will be

raised from the grave in preparation for the Day of Judgement.

2. To prove the truthfulness of our words, we need to rely on examples.
3. The best proof for the masses to believe in something is to present them with permanent, general, undeniable, and simple examples which are all around them to understand and witness.
4. One of the best ways to believe in and have a level of conviction in the Day of Resurrection is by carefully studying things around us – such as nature, the human body, etc.
5. A large part of what makes up the human food supply are the seeds which we put into the ground which grow into plants. By thoroughly considering this process, we can arrive at a deeper knowledge and cognizance of Allah ﷻ.

Part 16: The Blessings of Allah – Verses 34-35

وَجَعَلْنَا فِيهَا جَنَّٰتٍ مِّن نَّخِيلٍ وَأَعْنَٰبٍ وَفَجَّرْنَا فِيهَا مِنَ

ٱلْعُيُونِ ﴿٣٤﴾ لِيَأْكُلُوا۟ مِن ثَمَرِهِۦ وَمَا عَمِلَتْهُ أَيْدِيهِمْ ۚ أَفَلَا

يَشْكُرُونَ ﴿٣٥﴾

34. And We placed therein (on the earth) gardens of date-palms and grapevines, and We caused springs to gush forth from it.

35. So that they may enjoy its fruit, and that which their hands have worked for. Will they not then be grateful?

Thinking Points

Amongst all types of fruits, the ones which are most-often mentioned in the Quran are grapes and dates, and this may be due to the following reasons:

1. The role that these two fruits play in human food consumption.
2. The ease of accessibility of these two fruits for the people of the Arabian Peninsula – and even other regions of the world.
3. The fact that there are countless varieties of these two fruits.
4. These fruits can be consumed either fresh, dried, or preserved.

There could be several other reasons why Allah ﷻ specifically mentioned grapes and dates more than any other fruits in the Quran.

It should be noted that the two words used *'nakhīl'* which is translated as 'date-palm;' and *'a'nāb'* which is translated as 'grapevines' have been mentioned in the plural form in this verse because both dates and grapes come in diverse types and forms.[39]

Take Away Messages

1. When it comes to human food consumption and maintaining a healthy diet, the Quran seems to stress that importance should first be given to legumes, and then to naturally grown products, such as fruits.
2. It is imperative that a person recognizes and acknowledges that all the blessings they have are from Allah ﷻ, and one must be thankful for them. Allah ﷻ gives life to the dead earth, and through this process, He also provides plants, fruits, vegetables, and other things which we consume available to us. Thus, we must acknowledge Him and thank Him for these and all other innumerable blessings He continuously bestows upon us.
3. The production of diverse types of fruits is something which is explicitly noted in the Quran.

---

[39] Scientists have noted that there are over 600 varieties of dates, while there are over 10,000 varieties of grapes grown worldwide.

4. The expression that people use, even those who do not believe in the One True God, 'God-given blessings,' is something which should create a spirit of gratitude within us.

Part 17: Creation of Pairs – Verse 36

سُبْحَٰنَ ٱلَّذِى خَلَقَ ٱلْأَزْوَٰجَ كُلَّهَا مِمَّا تُنۢبِتُ ٱلْأَرْضُ وَمِنْ أَنفُسِهِمْ
وَمِمَّا لَا يَعْلَمُونَ ﴿٣٦﴾

36. Glory be to Him Who created pairs of all types of things that the earth grows, and from themselves, and from the things they do not yet know.

Thinking Points

One of the scientific miracles of the Quran is how it mentioned the universal law that everything has been created in pairs – plants, human beings, and even that which people did not know at the time when the Quran was being revealed, but today they know through the advancement of science and technology.[40]

---

[40] Does this verse of the Quran contradict scientific data on reproduction and 'pairs' of there being a male/female for all creations for reproduction to take place?

Modern biology recognizes that not all organisms reproduce in pairs. Some species reproduce asexually – such as bacteria (binary fission), plants (budding, fragmentation), and some animals (parthenogenesis).

In addition, the binary male-female distinction is not universal. Some species are hermaphroditic, possessing both male and female reproductive organs, and some can even change sex. As such, pairing is common, but not universal. Sexual reproduction

In the era of the revelation of the Quran, people were familiar with the date-palm tree and that they were dioecious – a tree that has either a male or female flower, however, today it is known that trees can either be dioecious, which refers to a tree that has **either** male or female flowers, while others are monoecious which are trees that have **both** male and female flowers.

---

involving two distinct individuals is widespread, but not the only mode of reproduction on Earth.

So, how can we reconcile the verse with modern scientific data?

We should note that the verse's language is broad and nuanced. The Arabic word *azwāj* (pairs) can refer to a wide range of dualities or complementary elements – not just male and female in the reproductive sense. In addition, the phrase "from things you do not (yet) know" suggests the verse is not limited to observable pairs but alludes to unknown or subtle forms of duality and complementarity in creation.

Further to this, the interpretations could be beyond biological sex. By this we mean that when we speak about pairs in Nature, we understand that dualities exist not only in living things, but also in non-living systems (e.g., positive/negative charges, matter/anti-matter).

In addition, we can take this verse in its philosophical/metaphorical reading which is that this verse can be understood as highlighting the principle of diversity, balance, and complementarity in creation, rather than making a strict biological claim about all species. (Tr.)

Take Away Messages

1. Our showing and expressing thanks to Allah ﷻ is a sign of our own spiritual growth. We should realize that He has no need for our thanks and accolades – it is us who need to thank Him for all that He has done for us and provided for us.
2. We must **never** apply the law of having a partner of the opposite gender which is seen in the world of creation to Allah ﷻ – for surely, He is One and Unique – with no need for a partner or child.
3. The power to create, and the existence of creations is a sign of the Power, Intention, and Wisdom of Allah ﷻ; it is **not** a sign of His needing anything, or that He is related to His creations.
4. The germination of a seed and its growth into a fruit is through the law of having two opposite genders which allows for plant reproduction.
5. When it comes to our physical needs and sexual desires, the human being is just like any other creation – we too require food, drink, and sexual relations to survive as a species.
6. There are still entities in the world whose pairing with one another is not yet known to human beings.

Part 18: Sun, Moon, Night, and Day – Verses 37-40

وَءَايَةٌ لَّهُمُ ٱلَّيْلُ نَسْلَخُ مِنْهُ ٱلنَّهَارَ فَإِذَا هُم مُّظْلِمُونَ ﴿٣٧﴾ وَٱلشَّمْسُ
تَجْرِى لِمُسْتَقَرٍّ لَّهَا ۚ ذَٰلِكَ تَقْدِيرُ ٱلْعَزِيزِ ٱلْعَلِيمِ ﴿٣٨﴾ وَٱلْقَمَرَ قَدَّرْنَٰهُ
مَنَازِلَ حَتَّىٰ عَادَ كَٱلْعُرْجُونِ ٱلْقَدِيمِ ﴿٣٩﴾ لَا ٱلشَّمْسُ يَنۢبَغِى لَهَآ أَن
تُدْرِكَ ٱلْقَمَرَ وَلَا ٱلَّيْلُ سَابِقُ ٱلنَّهَارِ ۚ وَكُلٌّ فِى فَلَكٍ يَسْبَحُونَ ﴿٤٠﴾

37. And a sign for them is the night. We remove from it the (light of) day, so they are (left) in darkness.

38. And the sun is moving (on its ordained course) towards the term appointed for it. That is the decree of the All-Mighty, the All-Knowing.

39. And the moon, We have determined for it phases, until it returns (to the stage when it appears) like an old dry twig of a palm-tree.

40. It is not permitted for the sun to reach the moon, nor can the night outstrip the day. All of these (luminaries) are floating (swimming) smoothly in an orbit (of their own).

Thinking Points

The word '*'urjūn*' which was translated as the 'dry twig of a palm-tree' is a part of the cluster of dates which is attached to the palm-tree, and over the course of time as it grows and matures, becomes arched in shape.

From these verses, the Proof of Order *(Burhān al-Nazm)* is established, which is one of the proofs of the existence of Allah ﷻ.

In addition:

1. The people's focus and attention to the movement of the sun and the moon.
2. The occurrence of night and day.
3. The changes seen in the phases of the moon.
4. The floating of celestial bodies such as the planets, stars, etc., and their orbits, and the fact that they do not collide with one another.

and all other precise scientific measurements which are observed in the system of creation are indications on the focus of Islam and the Quran on the need to study the universe, and to lay down a suitable framework for scientific research and study throughout history.

Take Away Messages

1. Night and day are signs of the Power and Wisdom of Allah ﷻ – one can only imagine if Earth were such that either one of the two (night or day) were to remain for 24 hours straight. To better appreciate how life would be radically altered, we can study regions such as Northern Canada, or the Scandinavian countries that have to deal with extremely lengthy day-light periods in the summer in which some areas have no nighttime; or those regions

which in the winter months, have little to no sunlight for large parts of the winter season.

2. The fixed program of how the celestial bodies move which has been in existence for the entire course of human history with no break in how it functions is a sign of the existence of a Wise and Supreme Creator who determines **everything** – Allah ﷻ.

3. The occurrence of night and day is not a coincidence, or a random event that started by chance – it is all according to the decree of Allah ﷻ.

4. The orbits of the sun and the moon are designed to never interfere with one another – they complement one another and all life on Earth.

5. Contrary to the theory that the sun is stationary, the Quran considers the sun to be moving, and it refers to it as a directional movement.

6. Absolutely no one can disturb the order which governs over all of existence – whatever Allah ﷻ has put into motion cannot be undone – other than by Him.

7. The similitudes of the Quran will never get old; the 'movement' of the moon through its various phases has been compared to the 'movement' – or better yet – the growth of the date-palm tree.

8. All the various celestial bodies in the universe are moving in their own orbit – determined and set into motion by Allah ﷻ.

9. The movement of objects such as the moon, sun, and planets around their own axis is being carried out at an extremely fast speed, and this can be best understood from the one word which the Quran uses in the verses under review – *'yasbaḥūn'* – which means 'swimming at a fast pace.'

Part 19: Means of Transport – Verses 41-44

وَءَايَةٌ لَّهُمْ أَنَّا حَمَلْنَا ذُرِّيَّتَهُمْ فِى ٱلْفُلْكِ ٱلْمَشْحُونِ ﴿٤١﴾ وَخَلَقْنَا لَهُم
مِّن مِّثْلِهِۦ مَا يَرْكَبُونَ ﴿٤٢﴾ وَإِن نَّشَأْ نُغْرِقْهُمْ فَلَا صَرِيخَ لَهُمْ وَلَا
هُمْ يُنقَذُونَ ﴿٤٣﴾ إِلَّا رَحْمَةً مِّنَّا وَمَتَٰعًا إِلَىٰ حِينٍ ﴿٤٤﴾

41. And a sign for them is that We carried their offspring in the (fully) laden ships.

42. And We created for them from the likes of it that which they ride.

43. And if We (so) willed, We would drown them, then they would have no (one to) respond to their cries, nor would they be saved.

44. It is only through mercy from Us (that We save them), and (let them have) an enjoyment (of worldly gains) for a while.

The use of ships and animals as a means of transportation has been repeatedly mentioned in the Quran, and they are regarded as being blessings from Allah ﷻ. However, in this verse, they are specifically mentioned as a means of carrying a person's offspring from place to place – perhaps so that people with wisdom and affection for their family will begin to reflect on the Divine blessings at a deeper level, and not just that they use these things to carry commodities to sell in the markets.

Today, human life would become paralyzed if the tankers which carry oil, wheat, food, and other products could not traverse in the oceans going from one country to another; and of course, transportation of cargo by sea is the cheapest way to move bulky goods.

Take Away Messages

1. Allah ﷻ created water in such a way that human beings can move on it through constructing ships – and this is one of the signs of the Power and Wisdom of Allah ﷻ.

2. A transportation vehicle – which is one of the necessities of human life – is a special blessing and sign of the Divine Grace of Allah ﷻ, and He designed this for us – whether it be a ship, horse, camel, car, or plane.

3. The proverbial Hand of Allah ﷻ – meaning His Power – is spread wide open when it comes to His Wrath and Anger. Thus, we must never be proud of ourselves and what we have created, or else we may end up being the recipients of His Divine Chastisement.

4. We should never consider our safety to be something which we have achieved through our own material accomplishments. The ships which traverse the oceans could sink at any moment were it not for the Mercy of Allah ﷻ – just as the planes that we construct which fly from country to country over the oceans could easily 'fall out of the sky' were it not for the continuous blessings of Allah ﷻ.

5. Everyone has an appointed term in this world, and one's life span is limited.

Part 20: Rejection of Messengers – Verses 45-46

وَإِذَا قِيلَ لَهُمُ ٱتَّقُواْ مَا بَيْنَ أَيْدِيكُمْ وَمَا خَلْفَكُمْ لَعَلَّكُمْ
تُرْحَمُونَ ﴿٤٥﴾ وَمَا تَأْتِيهِم مِّنْ ءَايَةٍ مِّنْ ءَايَٰتِ رَبِّهِمْ إِلَّا كَانُواْ عَنْهَا
مُعْرِضِينَ ﴿٤٦﴾

45. And when it is said to them: 'Guard yourselves against that (punishment) which is before you, and that which is behind you (because of your evil past), so that perhaps you may be shown mercy.'

46. And no sign comes to them from the signs of their Lord except that they turn away from it.

Thinking Points

In the previous verses, the Quran referenced some of the blessings of Allah ﷻ, and if the readers of the Quran were paying close attention, then they would realize that these gifts are indications of the Power, Wisdom, and Grace of Allah ﷻ.

In the verses under review, we are told that obstinate people do not take lessons from what they see around them, nor do they listen to wise admonition. Therefore, when it is said to them that they should keep away from performing those actions which may have retribution in this world and will have a punishment associated with them in the world to come, rather than humbling themselves so that they can be graced with the forgiveness of Allah ﷻ, they simply turn away and reject this!

Take Away Messages

1. It is through encouraging good *(amr bil maʿrūf)* that we can complete the proof *(itmām al-ḥujjah)* over humanity.
2. Having consciousness of Allah ﷻ *(taqwā)* is the secret to receiving His Divine Mercy.
3. To complete the proof, we must make use of various means.
4. The signs of Allah ﷻ are many, and they are sufficient for anyone seeking to find God, however, the people who study, acknowledge, and accept them are very few indeed.

Part 21: Spend Your Wealth Wisely – Verse 47

وَإِذَا قِيلَ لَهُمْ أَنفِقُوا۟ مِمَّا رَزَقَكُمُ ٱللَّهُ قَالَ ٱلَّذِينَ كَفَرُوا۟ لِلَّذِينَ
ءَامَنُوٓا۟ أَنُطْعِمُ مَن لَّوْ يَشَآءُ ٱللَّهُ أَطْعَمَهُۥٓ إِنْ أَنتُمْ إِلَّا فِى ضَلَـٰلٍ
مُّبِينٍ ﴿٤٧﴾

47. And when it is said to them: 'Spend out of that which Allah has provided for you,' those who disbelieve say to those who believe: 'Shall we feed those whom, if Allah so Wills, He could feed? You are not but in clear error.'

Thinking Points

There are people who do not have the right insight into life and want the burden of responsibility to be shifted away from them. They will even cast their deviant thoughts onto others. The Quran attests to this numerous times in various verses such as in the following examples:

1. Sometimes, they say: "Allah is guilty – if He did not Will for this to happen, then we would not have been among the polytheists." This ideology can be seen in the following verse: "If Allah had (so) Willed we would not have associated partners (with Him)"[41] and "If the All-

[41] Quran, Sūrah al-Anʿām (6), Verse 148:

Merciful had Willed, we would not have worshipped them (other than Allah ﷻ)."[42]

2. Sometimes they say: 'The society is to blame – if it was not for influential people, we would have become believers.' This is seen in the following verse: "Had it not been for you, we would surely have been believers."[43]
3. At other times they say: 'It is our forefathers who are to blame.' The Quran articulates this as follows: "Indeed, we found our fathers on this path."[44]

In this verse under review, we read similar excuses from those who do not want to adhere to the laws of the Almighty where they are quoted as saying: "If Allah wished, He could have fed all of the poor and needy people." However, individuals who make such baseless statements are ignorant of the fact that Allah ﷻ has placed the responsibility of feeding the poor on our shoulders to test us.

﴿...لَوْ شَآءَ ٱللَّهُ مَا أَشْرَكْنَا﴾

[42] Quran, Sūrah al-Zukhruf (43), Verse 20:

﴿...لَوْ شَآءَ ٱلرَّحْمَٰنُ مَا عَبَدْنَاهُم﴾

[43] Quran, Sūrah Saba' (34), Verse 31:

﴿لَوْلَآ أَنتُمْ لَكُنَّا مُؤْمِنِينَ﴾

[44] Quran, Sūrah al-Zukhruf (43), Verse 22:

﴿بَلْ قَالُوٓا۟ إِنَّا وَجَدْنَآ ءَابَآءَنَا عَلَىٰٓ أُمَّةٍ وَإِنَّا عَلَىٰٓ ءَاثَٰرِهِم مُّهْتَدُونَ﴾

Question: Why is it that Allah ﷻ Himself does not just give the poor people their sustenance, rather, He has ordered humanity to help them out?

Answer: Human growth takes place under the shadow of forgiveness, sacrifice, generosity, kindness, showing sympathy, being conscientious of the needs of others, love, cooperation, and affection for one another. If everyone had the same abilities, then there would not remain any grounds for an individual to develop these traits of human perfection within themselves, and there would be no means for the development of patience, serenity, and contentment for those who have been deprived.

For this reason, and since life is a test, we see that humanity is divided into two general categories: the 'haves' and the 'have-nots' – and it is up to each group to deal with the life they find themselves in using the qualities which Allah ﷻ has given them, and the guidance provided through His Prophets, Messengers, and Books.

Take Away Messages

1. If we keep in mind the fact that everything we have is from Allah ﷻ, and that in essence, everything belongs to Him and nothing is our own personal property, then it makes it easier to donate the excess of what we have been blessed by Allah ﷻ, and to give a helping hand to others who are less fortunate.

2. Disbelief *(kufr)* can lead a person to not give charity.

3. A disbeliever *(kāfir)* denies and laughs at the fact that Allah ﷻ is the true Provider. They think that they themselves have gotten to their state based on their own efforts.
4. Giving in charity is a sign of true faith *(īmān)*, while refraining from giving in charity is one of the signs of the disbelievers *(kuffār)*.
5. A person can reach a state where disbelief and stinginess become the 'right path' for them, and faith and charity are considered as being 'deviations.'

Part 22: Death and the Resurrection – Verses 48-50

وَيَقُولُونَ مَتَىٰ هَٰذَا ٱلْوَعْدُ إِن كُنتُمْ صَٰدِقِينَ ﴿٤٨﴾ مَا يَنظُرُونَ إِلَّا
صَيْحَةً وَٰحِدَةً تَأْخُذُهُمْ وَهُمْ يَخِصِّمُونَ ﴿٤٩﴾ فَلَا يَسْتَطِيعُونَ تَوْصِيَةً
وَلَآ إِلَىٰٓ أَهْلِهِمْ يَرْجِعُونَ ﴿٥٠﴾

48. And they (the disbelievers) say: 'When is this promise, if you are truthful?'

49. They do not wait except one blast which will seize them while they are disputing.

50. And they will not be able to give any instructions, nor to their own people will they return.

Thinking Points

Not only did the belligerent people mock Allah ﷻ, His Messengers and the message, but the disbelievers would go a step further and ridicule the Day of Resurrection. Thus, in this section, the Quran responds to their attacks by providing a decisive answer to such individuals.

The detractors began another line of questioning about the Day of Resurrection by doubting when that Day will occur. They pressed Prophet Muḥammad ﷺ – just as the people of the past also rudely asked their own Messengers – that if the Day of Judgement is a reality, and the message of the

Prophets is truthful, then they should be able to tell the society when the promised Day will arrive.

The disbelievers felt that if these men of Allah ﷻ could not set a specific date for when the Resurrection will occur, then this means they are not honest in their speech and invitation as they should know such things.

The verses under review provide a strong, yet solemn response, mixed with a touch of sarcasm – as Allah ﷻ occasionally does in the Quran. In this passage, the Quran responds and says that the beginning of the Day of Resurrection, and thus, the end of this world, is not a complicated issue for Allah ﷻ to initiate. Obstinate people will be disputing with one another even as this event begins to transpire!

This one massive event will be enough to stop everything and take everyone's existence in an instant; and their busy, material life, which was a constant arena of activity, will all come to a screeching halt.

In one *ḥadīth*, Prophet Muḥammad ﷺ has described this Day as being so intense and instantaneous that if two people were involved in a business transaction in which the seller was selling a piece of fabric and the one was about to stretch it open for the client to see, before they even have time to do that, the world will come to an end without them being able to finalize the deal – that is the speed and severity with which this world will end!

In the same *ḥadīth*, Prophet Muḥammad ﷺ went on to say that there will be people who would have just lifted a morsel of food from their plate, but before the food could reach their mouth, the Heavenly Noise which heralds the end of this world will arrive, and they will not even have the time to put that last bite of food in their mouth.

In the last part of this *ḥadīth*, Prophet Muḥammad ﷺ is noted as saying that if there was a person who was busy in repairing and lining the reservoir of water in the front yard of their house with mud so that their animals would have a well from which they could drink water, and the Day of Judgement were to arrive, the man will not be able to complete the building of the well, and his animals will not have an opportunity to take their first sip of water from the watering hole being built for them – both the animals and the owner will die in that sorrowful state.[45]

The verses under review mention that the Day of Judgement will come. In this scene however, it mentions that people will be disputing with one another – but about what will they be arguing?

Based on what we know about their lifestyles and disregard for matters of faith, their arguments usually surround some aspect of this material world – business, entertainment, etc. – areas that people normally argue about or have passionate discussions regarding. Sometimes these heated chats resemble disputes but are just obsessive chats –

---

[45] *Tafsīr Majmaʿ al-Bayān:*

تَقُومُ السَّاعَةُ وَالرَّجُلَانِ قَدْ نَشَرَا ثَوْبَهُمَا يَتَبَايَعَانِهِ فَمَا يَطْوِيَانِهِ حَتَّى تَقُومَ! وَالرَّجُلُ يَرْفَعُ أُكْلَتَهُ إِلَى فِيْهِ فَمَا تَصِلُ إِلَى فِيهِ حَتَّى تَقُومَ! وَالرَّجُلُ يَلِيطُ حَوْضَهُ لِيَسْقِيَ مَاشِيَتَهُ فَمَا يَسْقِيهَا حَتَّى تَقُومَ.

many times about trivial matters such as a person's favourite sports team, or a recent sporting event.

We should bear in mind that although these verses are speaking about people at the time of Prophet Muḥammad ﷺ, and even those who came in the past and disputed with their respective Prophets, however, they are not limited to the past era. Even in our time, and as we get closer to the end of this world, these same discussions and arguments about the Day of Judgement will come up.

Usually, when a person goes through an accident and they feel that the end of their life is drawing near, one of the things they want to do, regardless of whether they are believers in God or not is to go back to their home. They want to be surrounded by those things which bring them comfort – their physical home, their belongings, their families, etc. They want to be around such people to pass on any last requests and spend their final few moments in their presence.

However, the end of this world will not allow them or anyone that opportunity.

As noted, this event will come about so rapidly that no one will be able to do anything – not even sit and draft their last will and testament or leave any requests for their families. They will not even have an opportunity to return to their home to be with their family in those last moments.

Even if the person did not want to dictate their last requests, at least they would hope to lie on their bed with their family around them; for their family to console them, hug them, give them the peace of mind and comfort they need as they pass on from this world.

However, as the Quran reiterates in this passage, none of this will be possible.

Take Away Messages

1. The disbelievers have no proof for the **denial** of the resurrection, so it is only through raising the question of **when** the resurrection will take place that they seek to mock it.
2. Just because something is not exactly specified as to **when** it will occur, this **does not negate its occurrence**, and it is not proof that it will not transpire either.
3. The Resurrection and Day of Accountability are a promise of Allah ﷻ.
4. The disbelievers consider the Prophets sent by Allah ﷻ and the true believers as being liars.
5. The Resurrection will not necessarily announce itself that it is arriving – so why are people in a state of spiritual negligence and mockery of that Day?
6. Once the Resurrection begins, neither will the tongue be able to speak, nor will the feet be able to flee from it!
7. The resurrection of humanity will begin after a death-inducing sound is signaled.
8. The end of this temporal world and the beginning of the Day of Resurrection will take place at a time when people will be busy with their daily lives. This means that people will be busy with whatever keeps them preoccupied, and

with the blowing of the trumpet, all life will end. Then after some period, the trumpet will be blown again to bring everyone back to life – recreated – to stand in the Court of Justice of Allah ﷻ.

9. In this temporal world, there are dependencies and enslavements upon things and other people, however, with the Resurrection and Day of Judgement, all these ties and relationships will be broken.

Part 23: The End of this World – Verses 51-53

وَنُفِخَ فِي ٱلصُّورِ فَإِذَا هُم مِّنَ ٱلۡأَجۡدَاثِ إِلَىٰ رَبِّهِمۡ يَنسِلُونَ ۝٥١ قَالُواْ
يَٰوَيۡلَنَا مَنۢ بَعَثَنَا مِن مَّرۡقَدِنَاۜۗ هَٰذَا مَا وَعَدَ ٱلرَّحۡمَٰنُ وَصَدَقَ
ٱلۡمُرۡسَلُونَ ۝٥٢ إِن كَانَتۡ إِلَّا صَيۡحَةٗ وَٰحِدَةٗ فَإِذَا هُمۡ جَمِيعٞ لَّدَيۡنَا
مُحۡضَرُونَ ۝٥٣

51. And the trumpet shall be blown, and at once they will hasten from their graves to their Lord.

52. They will say (to one another): 'O woe be upon us! Who has raised us up from our sleeping place?' (They will receive the reply) This is what the All-Merciful (Allah) had promised, and the Messengers (of Allah) indeed spoke the truth.'

53. It will not be but a single blast, and at once they will all be brought before Us.

Thinking Points

In the Quran, it has been mentioned that the trumpet which will bring about an end to all in existence will be blown twice:

1. First time to herald the end of this world.
2. Second time to initiate the Day of Resurrection.

The meaning of 'the trumpet shall be blown' in the first verse under review is the second blowing of the trumpet which will bring life again to everyone in existence, thus initiating the resurrection from the graves.

There are some key words in this passage which we should reflect upon:

1. The word '*ajdāth*' is the plural of '*jadath*' which means 'the grave.'
2. The word '*yansilūn*' comes from the word '*nislān*' and it means 'to move with haste.'
3. The word '*marqad*' is the Noun of the Place (*al-Ism al-Makān*) and comes from the word '*riqād*' which means 'the place of resting,' thus in this context, it refers to 'the grave.'

Imam Muḥammad al-Bāqir ﷺ said: "In regard to the portion of the verse which reads: 'This is what the All-Merciful had promised, and the Messengers (of Allah ﷻ) indeed spoke the truth,' this will be the speech of the angels with the people who are all gathered on the plains of the Day of Judgement."[46]

Take Away Messages

1. The beginning of the Day of Resurrection will take place with a sound which will be created through blowing into a trumpet, and it will be heard by all creations.

2. The resurrection is physical, and the bodies of all of humanity will come out of the same graves in which they were buried.

---

[46] *Tafsīr Nūr al-Thaqalayn.*

3. Human beings will be brought back to life on the Day of Resurrection extremely quickly and with great ease – for everything is 'simple' for Allah ﷻ to perform.
4. The reason for moving with great haste is a sign of the distress and confusion which everyone will face on the Day of Judgement.
5. The Day of Resurrection will be one of great regret and remorse for the disbelievers and wrongdoers.
6. The resurrection will be a scene of spiritual awakening, confirmation, and confession.
7. The setting up of the Day of Resurrection and Accountability is a requirement to display the Mercy and Justice of Allah ﷻ.
8. On the Day of Judgement, all of humanity will be presented in one gathering.
9. Being present on the Plains of Resurrection is not something which we have a choice about deciding whether we want to show up there or not, it is a reality that everyone will have to be present for.

Part 24: Infinite Justice of Allah – Verse 54

فَٱلْيَوْمَ لَا تُظْلَمُ نَفْسٌ شَيْـًٔا وَلَا تُجْزَوْنَ إِلَّا مَا كُنتُمْ تَعْمَلُونَ ﴿٥٤﴾

54. So, on this Day no injustice whatsoever shall be done to any soul; and you will not be compensated except for what you used to do.

Thinking Points

This verse explains the concept of the **Physical Manifestations** ***(Tajassum al-Aʿmāl)*** in which our actions performed in this world will take a form on the Day of Judgement. This verse tells us: Your rewards will be based upon nothing other than your own actions, and therefore it says: 'What you used to do' or in other words: 'You shall reap the returns of your deeds.'

If this verse had read: 'You shall reap the returns **because** of your deeds,' that is, with the addition of the letter *bā'* before the word *mā'* (thus, if it said بِـمَا), then it would have meant that people will receive a reward or punishment **because** they acted in this world – either acting righteously or wickedly.

Thus, there is a vast difference between both interpretations, however, since Allah ﷻ DID NOT use the letter *bā'*, we derive the first meaning provided for this verse – which is that we will be rewarded or given a retribution based on own actions in this world.

Take Away Messages

1. Allah ﷻ is Just *(al-ʿĀdil)*, and the Day of Judgement is a time when the complete manifestation and demonstration of the Justice of Allah ﷻ will take place. It should be noted that even the most challenging types of punishments will be met with justice by the Almighty.
2. The retributions and rewards on Judgement Day will be given to us according to the actions we performed in this transient world and are based on the scales of fairness of Allah ﷻ.

Part 25: The Pleasures of Paradise – Verses 55-58

إِنَّ أَصْحَٰبَ ٱلْجَنَّةِ ٱلْيَوْمَ فِى شُغُلٍ فَٰكِهُونَ ٥٥ هُمْ وَأَزْوَٰجُهُمْ فِى
ظِلَٰلٍ عَلَى ٱلْأَرَآئِكِ مُتَّكِـُٔونَ ٥٦ لَهُمْ فِيهَا فَٰكِهَةٌ وَلَهُم مَّا
يَدَّعُونَ ٥٧ سَلَٰمٌ قَوْلًا مِّن رَّبٍّ رَّحِيمٍ ٥٨

55. Indeed, the companions of Paradise on this Day will be occupied (in their pursuits), rejoicing.

56. They and their spouses will be in (pleasant) shades, reclining on (raised) couches.

57. Therein they shall have fruits, and they will have all that they request.

58. 'Peace' a word from a Merciful Lord.

Thinking Points

We should reflect on the following important words which Allah ﷻ uses in this passage:

1. The word *'shugul'* means 'something which keeps a person busy.'
2. The word *'fākhihūn'* comes from the word *'fakāhah'* which means 'speech that brings about happiness.'
3. The word *'arā'ik'* is the plural of *'arīka'* and it refers to 'an ornate throne or couch which is in the room of a bride.'

One of the things which will be prominent in Paradise is that there will be peace *(salām)* from all directions, thus Allah ﷻ says in the Quran in various places:

1. Allah ﷻ will address the people with the phrase '*salām*' – as we read – "'Peace,' a word from a Merciful Lord."[47]
2. The angels will also convey their greetings of '*salām*' – "...And the angels will come to them from every gate, (saying): 'Peace be upon you, for that you endured patiently. How excellent is the ultimate everlasting abode!'"[48]
3. The people of Paradise will also greet one another with the phrase '*salām*' – "...And their greeting (to each other and from Allah ﷻ and the angels) will be: 'Peace!'"[49]

---

[47] Quran, Sūrah Yāsīn (36), Verse 58.

[48] Quran, Sūrah al-Raʿd (13), Verses 23-24:

﴿جَنَّٰتُ عَدۡنٖ يَدۡخُلُونَهَا وَمَن صَلَحَ مِنۡ ءَابَآئِهِمۡ وَأَزۡوَٰجِهِمۡ وَذُرِّيَّٰتِهِمۡۖ وَٱلۡمَلَٰٓئِكَةُ يَدۡخُلُونَ
عَلَيۡهِم مِّن كُلِّ بَابٖ ٢٣ سَلَٰمٌ عَلَيۡكُم بِمَا صَبَرۡتُمۡۚ فَنِعۡمَ عُقۡبَى ٱلدَّارِ ٢٤﴾

[49] Quran, Sūrah Yūnus (10), Verse 10:

﴿دَعۡوَىٰهُمۡ فِيهَا سُبۡحَٰنَكَ ٱللَّهُمَّ وَتَحِيَّتُهُمۡ فِيهَا سَلَٰمٞۚ وَءَاخِرُ دَعۡوَىٰهُمۡ أَنِ ٱلۡحَمۡدُ لِلَّهِ رَبِّ
ٱلۡعَٰلَمِينَ ١٠﴾

Take Away Messages

1. In Paradise, there will be no concept of 'laziness' – the word used in the passage of verses under review, *'shughulin,'* with the nunation *(tanwīn)* at the end of it, as well as it being the indefinite noun *(nakira),* gives it the meaning of 'some activity whose depths are unknown, and something which is indescribable.'
2. In Paradise, there will be no grief or sorrow of any kind.
3. Paradise will see:
    a. Life without death.
    b. Health without sickness.
    c. Youth without aging.
    d. Respect without humiliation.
    e. Abundant blessings given without any effort.
    f. Existence without annihilation.
    g. Happiness without anger.
    h. Fondness without fear.
4. In Paradise, there will be no loneliness.
5. The places of abode in Paradise will grant everyone who goes there, comfort and tranquility.
6. Sitting on couches and chairs is favoured to sitting on the floor.

7. The best types of foods will exist in Paradise – in this verse, the word *'fākihatun'* which means 'fruits' is mentioned as an indefinite noun *(nakira)* indicating that when people enter Paradise, one of the first things they will be given is various fruits.

8. There will be no limits in Paradise – the word *'yaddaʿūn'* means that 'whatever people want, and desire will be given to them.'

9. Resurrection is a physical event, and our lives in the next world will also be physical; and the words used in this verse such as fruits, spouses, and couches show us that the resurrection will take place with similar physical bodies which we currently have.

10. It is in Paradise where people will experience the true pleasure and peace of the Greatness of Allah ﷻ.

11. Receiving peace from Allah ﷻ is a wish and desire that all the people of Paradise will yearn for.

Part 26: Sinners and their Ending – Verses 59-62

وَٱمْتَـٰزُوا۟ ٱلْيَوْمَ أَيُّهَا ٱلْمُجْرِمُونَ ﴿٥٩﴾ أَلَمْ أَعْهَدْ إِلَيْكُمْ يَـٰبَنِىٓ ءَادَمَ
أَن لَّا تَعْبُدُوا۟ ٱلشَّيْطَـٰنَ ۖ إِنَّهُۥ لَكُمْ عَدُوٌّ مُّبِينٌ ﴿٦٠﴾ وَأَنِ ٱعْبُدُونِى ۚ
هَـٰذَا صِرَٰطٌ مُّسْتَقِيمٌ ﴿٦١﴾ وَلَقَدْ أَضَلَّ مِنكُمْ جِبِلًّا كَثِيرًا ۖ أَفَلَمْ
تَكُونُوا۟ تَعْقِلُونَ ﴿٦٢﴾

59. And (it will be said to the sinners): 'O guilty ones! Stand apart today.

60. Did I not enjoin upon you not to (ever) worship Satan, for surely, he is to you an open enemy.

61. And (did I not instruct you) to (only) worship Me, (for) this is the Straight Path?

62. And he (Satan) certainly led astray several people from among you. Why do you then not make use of your reason?'

Thinking Points

The separation of the sinners from the righteous people will be something carried out according to the Law of Justice of Allah ﷻ, just as He has mentioned in another verse of the

Quran: "(What!?) Then is one who was a believer like one who is defiantly disobedient? They can never be equal."[50]

In addition, it is possible that the meaning of there being a differentiation between these two groups is that the guilty sinners will be separated from each other and kept all on their own, thus also feeling the pain of separation and isolation from one another.

Sometimes, one of the worst forms of punishment is when a person is secluded from others. Thus, we see that in the world today, sometimes prisoners are kept in solitary confinement away from other people, and many of them attest that not having any human interaction is one of the worst forms of cruel and unusual punishment they can be given.

The phrase *'jibilan kathīran'* is used to refer to 'many people who are just like a huge mountain.'[51]

The meaning of the phrase 'not to (ever) worship Satan' – as has also been mentioned in the *ḥadīth* – means: "A person who obeys another in disobedience to the rules of Allah ﷻ has surely worshipped them."[52] Thus, this phrase as used in

---

[50] Quran, Sūrah al-Sajdah (32), Verse 18:

﴿أَفَمَنْ كَانَ مُؤْمِناً كَمَنْ كَانَ فَاسِقاً لاَ يَسْتَوُونَ﴾

[51] *Al-Mufradāt* of al-Rāghib.

[52] *Wasā'il al-Shī'a*, Vol. 18, Pg. 79. The Arabic of this tradition is as follows:

مَنْ أَطَاعَ رَجُلًا فِي مَعْصِيَةٍ فَقَدْ عَبَدَهُ.

the Quran does not refer to people who 'worship' Satan or pray at the altar of contemporary Satan-worshippers.

Take Away Messages

1. The Resurrection Day will be one of separation and estrangement.

2. Allah ﷻ – through the Prophets, the intellect *('aql)*, and the innate human disposition *(fiṭrah)* – took a pledge with all of humanity to submit to and worship only Him and turn away from all despots – all the Devils – whether from the *jinn* or humanity.

3. Satan was able to 'mislead' our father (Prophet Ādam عليه السلام), and as such, we are the children of that individual who 'was tricked' by Satan, so we need to be extra cautious not to be misguided by Satan during our life.

4. A human being is either a servant of Allah ﷻ or a servant of the Devil.

5. The fact that Satan is an open enemy for everyone is clear – and the mere thought that idols created from inanimate objects such as rocks and wood can take the place of Allah ﷻ and become a manifestation of Him is something which is a clear path of deviation that Satan has managed to get multitudes of people to accept and follow.

6. The Straight Path *(Ṣirāṭ al-Mustaqīm)* which we ask Allah ﷻ to guide us and keep us upon every day and night in our daily prayers (in the form of Sūrah al-Fātiḥa) is the path of obedience and worship of the Almighty Allah ﷻ.

7. We need to take lessons from individuals of the past who were misled and try our best **not** to follow them.
8. Thinking about the bitter outcome of those who had been misled by the guiles of Satan is one of the ways to save ourselves from the whispers and temptations of the Devil.

Part 27: Enter the Fires of Hell – Verses 63-64

هَٰذِهِۦ جَهَنَّمُ ٱلَّتِي كُنتُمۡ تُوعَدُونَ ﴿٦٣﴾ ٱصۡلَوۡهَا ٱلۡيَوۡمَ بِمَا كُنتُمۡ
تَكۡفُرُونَ ﴿٦٤﴾

63. 'This is the Hellfire which you were promised.

64. (Enter it to) burn therein today for what you used to deny.'

Thinking Points

The previous verses recounted some of the reprimands which Allah ﷻ will issue, and a portion of His conversations with the criminals on the Day of Resurrection. The verses under review in this section continue those discussions, however, look at them from another angle.

The Quran confirms that on that Day, the burning, blazing fire will be made present in front of the eyes of these criminals, and as if pointing towards it, Allah ﷻ will address the individuals destined for Hell and tell them that this is the Hellfire which they were all promised.

The word *'iṣlawhā'* is from the Arabic root *'ṣallā'* and it means 'to start a fire,' and the inherent understanding of it is also 'to enter a fire once it has been lit.'

Throughout the course of human history, Allah ﷻ continuously sent Prophets, Messengers, and others to help humanity arrive to and stay on the Straight Path. All the emissaries sent by Allah ﷻ also warned the people of a terrible punishment if they decided to disregard the Divine teachings and live carefree lives, devoid of Allah ﷻ.

As the people decided to reject His Message and Messengers, and commit crimes against themselves and oppress others, their only outcome is that on the Day of Judgement, after having all of their actions considered, they will have to suffer the fate they had been warned about.

Take Away Messages

1. On numerous occasions in the Quran, Allah ﷻ gives the promise of the fire of Hell – however, this is something which the disbelievers continuously deny.
2. Allah ﷻ completes the argument for those individuals who are bound for Hell, and in the Quran, continuously conveys to them the warning of the fire so that they may reflect on their lives and change their ways.
3. The entrance of the disbelievers into the fire of Hell will also be accompanied by them facing intense humiliation by the onlookers.
4. The disbelievers and those bound for the fire of Hell will never be spared from the fire of Allah ﷻ.

Part 28: Mouths will be Sealed – Verse 65

> ٱلْيَوْمَ نَخْتِمُ عَلَىٰٓ أَفْوَٰهِهِمْ وَتُكَلِّمُنَآ أَيْدِيهِمْ وَتَشْهَدُ أَرْجُلُهُم بِمَا كَانُوا۟ يَكْسِبُونَ ﴿٦٥﴾
>
> 65. On that Day, We shall seal over their mouths, and their hands will speak to Us (about the actions which they performed), and their feet will bear witness about what they earned.

Thinking Points

In this verse of the Quran, we see the mention of just two parts of the body: the hands and feet. This does not mean that the rest of the body will also not be considered for what it did.

Rather, these two are only presented to us in this passage to provide us with an example, as from other verses of the Quran we read that the ears, eyes, and heart will also be questioned: "Do not follow that of which you have no knowledge (whether it is good or bad), and refrain from groundless assertions and conjectures. Surely the hearing, the sight, and the heart – each of these is subject to questioning about it (you are answerable, and will be called to account, for each of these on the Day of Judgement)."[53]

---

[53] Quran, Sūrah al-Isrā' (17), Verse 36:

In another verse, we are told that even the skin will be called to testify: "Until when they reach it, their ears, and their eyes, and their skins will bear witness against them as to all that they did habitually."[54]

In any case, as we know, each body part will be made to bear witness as to the actions which it performed.

Take Away Messages

1. Allah ﷻ is the One who brings about the causes of everything which occurs and even what we say or do. The same mouth which was used to speak in this world will be sealed on that Day, and the hands and feet which could not talk in this life will be made to speak.
2. Resurrection is a physical event.
3. On the Day of Judgement, the parts of the body will not do what a person wants them to do. Rather, they will obey the commands of Allah ﷻ and do what they are told to do.

﴿وَلَا تَقْفُ مَا لَيْسَ لَكَ بِهِۦ عِلْمٌ ۚ إِنَّ ٱلسَّمْعَ وَٱلْبَصَرَ وَٱلْفُؤَادَ كُلُّ أُو۟لَٰٓئِكَ كَانَ عَنْهُ مَسْـُٔولًا ﴿٣٦﴾﴾

[54] Quran, Sūrah Fuṣṣilat (41), Verse 20:

﴿حَتَّىٰٓ إِذَا مَا جَآءُوهَا شَهِدَ عَلَيْهِمْ سَمْعُهُمْ وَأَبْصَٰرُهُمْ وَجُلُودُهُم بِمَا كَانُوا۟ يَعْمَلُونَ ﴿٢٠﴾﴾

4. The most powerful witnesses who will testify in court on the Day of Resurrection will be the body parts themselves that were made to perform sins.
5. Our body parts all have a form of understanding and perception and **can** and **will** testify on the Day of Judgement – for or against the human being.

Part 29: If Allah Wanted To... – Verses 66-67

وَلَوْ نَشَآءُ لَطَمَسْنَا عَلَىٰٓ أَعْيُنِهِمْ فَٱسْتَبَقُوا۟ ٱلصِّرَٰطَ فَأَنَّىٰ يُبْصِرُونَ
﴿٦٦﴾ وَلَوْ نَشَآءُ لَمَسَخْنَٰهُمْ عَلَىٰ مَكَانَتِهِمْ فَمَا ٱسْتَطَٰعُوا۟ مُضِيًّا وَلَا
يَرْجِعُونَ ﴿٦٧﴾

66. And if We had (so) willed, We could certainly have deprived these (disbelievers) of their eyesight so that they would have gone ahead on their path (not being able to see). But then, how would they find (the path) now (in that state of blindness).

67. And if We had (so) willed, We could have surely destroyed them where they were, so that they would not be able to move forward, nor turn back.

Thinking Points

If we consider these two verses as being a continuation of the two preceding verses about the punishment which will be met out to the disbelievers after the resurrection in the next world, then it indicates the helplessness of the disbelievers in seeking a way to get to Paradise, and their astonishment and wandering in the plains on the Day of Judgement.

However, most of the commentators of the Quran consider these two verses to be speaking about the worldly punishment of the disbelievers and consider them to be a form of warning about the loss of their vision and not being able to find their way back home, or to their workplace.[55]

Take Away Messages

1. People must not think that the things they have are because they are God's chosen people, or have been given extra privilege, or that they will have them forever. Also, people must not be negligent of the Wrath of Allah ﷻ, or the fact that blessings which He provides can be taken away at any time.
2. We must realize that prevention is better than cure. Therefore, before Divine punishment descends, we must ensure that we humble ourselves and remove any display of pride or obstinacy.
3. Any time and place, one can experience the Wrath of Allah ﷻ.
4. No one can bear the Wrath of Allah ﷻ when it occurs.
5. The Tradition of Allah ﷻ *(Sunnatullāh)* is that He allows humanity to be free to do as they wish. However, at the same time, He has given people the power of sight, hearing, and the intellect so that they may come to the truths of faith themselves, as He will never bring a person to the path of submission through compulsion or forced fear.

---

[55] *Tafsīr-e Nemunah.*

Part 30: A Reversal of Our Lives – Verse 68

وَمَن نُّعَمِّرْهُ نُنَكِّسْهُ فِي ٱلْخَلْقِ أَفَلَا يَعْقِلُونَ ۝٦٨

68. And the one to whom We grant long life; We reverse in creation; will they not then understand?

Thinking Points

In the previous verses, Allah ﷻ stated that: "If We willed, we would have blinded their eyes and altered their appearances," while the verse under review presents us with a sample of what this change could look like if it came down upon a person.

The word *'nunakkishu'* comes from the word *'tankīsun'* and it means 'overturning something,' however, in the context as it is used in this verse, it refers to 'a person being brought back to the state one was in as a child.'

In most cases, the knowledge and intellect of a person that is getting older eventually turns to forgetfulness; their strengths turn to weaknesses; and their patience and forbearance withers away and they become easily irritated. They are usually extremely sensitive and may even cry more than in their youthful days. When we look at the state of the seniors, we tend to see that many of the traits they exhibit in their old age mimic how a young child is – thus, confirming verses of the Quran.

Take Away Messages

1. Our lives are only in the Hands of Allah ﷻ – whether we age with grace or leave this world before making it to our senior years.

2. The Tradition of Allah ﷻ *(Sunnatullāh)* is that old age is accompanied by a breakdown of sorts, and this is best understood by the Quran making use of the phrase "And the one to whom We grant long life, We reverse them..." Although we should keep in mind that the effects of aging are all in the Hands of Allah ﷻ, and whatever Allah ﷻ decrees will happen, we see individuals such as Prophet Nūḥ ؑ and Imam al-Mahdī عجل الله فرجه الشريف – although both having extraordinarily long lives, they did not see this failure due to their age. We also witness that when it comes to certain great scholars of Islam and other pious individuals who live to be old, they do not lose their senses or end up being as Allah ﷻ describes in this verse.

3. Human beings should always think about the fact that they could lose Divine blessings at any time, and the words *'ṭamasna'* which means 'deprived,' and *'masakhnā'* which means 'destroyed' refer to the reality of getting old and frail – thus, losing the beautiful gifts of Allah ﷻ.

Part 31: The Prophet is not a Poet – Verse 69

وَمَا عَلَّمْنَٰهُ ٱلشِّعْرَ وَمَا يَنۢبَغِى لَهُۥٓ ۚ إِنْ هُوَ إِلَّا ذِكْرٌ وَقُرْءَانٌ مُّبِينٌ ﴿٦٩﴾

69. And We have not taught him (Prophet Muḥammad ﷺ, the art of composing) verses, nor is it befitting for him (to be a poet). It (the Quran) is not but a Reminder and a clear recitation.

Thinking Points

One of the baseless accusations which the disbelievers levelled against the final Messenger, Prophet Muḥammad ﷺ, in addition to calling him a magician, insane, and a sorcerer, was the accusation of him being a poet. Upon hearing the beautiful, powerful words of the Quran, the disbelievers of the Quraysh presumed Prophet Muḥammad ﷺ to be nothing more than a poet who was composing these words and passing them off as revelation.

However, Divine revelation *(Waḥī)* is quite different from poetry in that:

1. Poetry stems from one's imagination, whereas revelation is from Allah ﷻ.
2. Poetry comes about from emotions and sentiments, but Divine revelation is not dependent on how a person feels.

Although some of the sentences of the Quran contain balanced stanzas and line breaks which resemble Arabic poetry, one of the main factors in the creation of poetry is that it is heavily dependent on the usage of one's imagination, and this is not something which can ever be attributed to the Noble Quran.

Therefore, the Quran must be recognized just as Allah ﷻ has described – it is a Reminder *(Dhikr)* – and as we are told – This [the Quran] is nothing but:

1. A Reminder about the Power and Wrath of Allah ﷻ.
2. A Reminder about the never-ending Grace and Blessings of the Almighty.
3. A Reminder of His Forgiveness and Clemency.
4. A Reminder of His Immutable Constants – also referred to as the Traditions of Allah *(Sunnatullāh)*, and His overarching rules which govern everything.
5. A Reminder of His Prophets, Successors, and close friends – the *Awliyā'*.
6. A Reminder about the history of other nations which are full of lessons.
7. A Reminder about the reasons for the greatness and falls of various nations.
8. A Reminder of the good doers and those who received guidance.
9. A Reminder of those who were destroyed – the disbelievers, the open transgressors, the sinners, and the oppressors – and their eventual outcomes.
10. A Reminder about the people of sincerity, self-sacrifice, bravery, generosity, fortitude, and the outcome of all of those who were righteous individuals.

11. A Reminder of those who were killed, tortured, harassed, falsely accused, humiliated, had their rights taken away, and were considered weak and powerless, and the degrading outcome of the arrogant tyrants.
12. A Reminder of the commands, prohibitions, good exhortations, and wise council.
13. A Reminder about all the created things which exist in the skies, on the earth, and in the oceans.
14. A Reminder about the future and eventual victory of the government of truth, and the filling of this world with justice and equality, and the condemnation of oppression and tyranny.
15. A Reminder about the intermediary realm after death *(barzakh)*, Resurrection, the events which will transpire before the Day of Judgement, how the scenes will be on that dreadful Day, and how treacherous the things will be in Hell, and how beautiful the blessings of Paradise will be.

In short, the Quran is a clear Reminder for all of humankind regarding a countless number of things to reflect upon and take lessons from.

Take Away Messages

1. In the Quran, there is no mention of negating the value of poetry in general, rather the discussion focuses on the point of negating that these words of the Prophet ﷺ – which are the revealed words of the Quran – were **not** poetry, rather they were Divine revelation from Allah ﷻ to Prophet Muḥammad ﷺ.

2. Allah ﷻ defends His Prophets from false accusations levelled against them.

3. Contrary to widespread belief, if a person is a propagator of religion, that is, a *muballigh*, they are not rendered irrelevant or worthless if they do not know poetry.[56]

4. Misplaced societal progress, and a wrong cultural vision should not be confused with the proper culture of a society. At the time of Prophet Muḥammad ﷺ, poetry was at the top of the agenda for the masses. As such, poetry and poets were extremely important – but this verse sought to break this false sense of pride which existed among them.

5. The nature of poetry comes to us from Allah ﷻ.

6. The true teacher of Prophet Muḥammad ﷺ was Allah ﷻ Himself.

7. Not every science is fit for everyone to learn.

8. If we do not empty ourselves from the fantasies and dreams of a poet, then our soul will never be able to become a vessel for the teachings of the Divine.

---

[56] In some Eastern cultures, poetry makes up a great deal of their daily discourse; and thus, some religious scholars are not considered capable of lecturing if they have not memorized poetry in that language. Thus, if a person wants to be effective and make an impact on those communities, and wants the people to hear their message, they need to better themselves as it relates to memorizing and quoting poetry. (Tr.)

9. The Quran – which is a Reminder – is a repository of reminders.
10. The Quran is clear speech which can be understood easily, and it is a Divine Book of many manifest proofs.

Part 32: The Quran: A Book of Life – Verse 70

لِّيُنذِرَ مَن كَانَ حَيًّا وَيَحِقَّ ٱلْقَوْلُ عَلَى ٱلْكَٰفِرِينَ ﴿٧٠﴾

70. (The Quran has been revealed) so that he (the Prophet) may warn those who are still (somewhat spiritually) alive, (and capable of receiving and responding to the call of truth), and (that) the verdict (of condemnation) be justified against the disbelievers.

Thinking Points

The Quran shows us that life is of distinct types:

1. Vegetative Life: "...And He gives life to the earth after its death..."[57]
2. Animal Life – given that humans are a type of animal who came into existence and were given life by Allah ﷻ: "...When you were without life then He gave you life..."[58]
3. Intellectual Life: "...respond to Allah and the Messenger when he calls you to that which will give you life..."[59]

---

[57] Quran, Sūrah al-Rūm (30), Verse 19:

﴿يُحْيِي الْأَرْضَ بَعْدَ مَوْتِهَا﴾

[58] Quran, Sūrah al-Baqarah (2), Verse 28:

﴿كُنْتُمْ أَمْوَاتًا فَأَحْيَاكُمْ﴾

[59] Quran, Sūrah al-Anfāl (8), Verse 24:

4. Societal Life: "And there is life for you in the laws of retaliation..."[60]
5. Heart and Spiritual Life: "That it may give admonition to any (who are) alive..."[61]

The Quran is a Book of Guidance that will warn those individuals who have a spiritual heart which is alive and have a clean soul.

True believers are people whose spiritual hearts are alive, and are experiencing a true, noble life; while the disbelievers are individuals who are like the dead and are prevented from enjoying true life.

According to the traditions, the meaning of the word *'ḥayyan'* – 'living' are 'those who have intellect.'[62]

The issue of the definite Wrath of Allah ﷻ which will affect the disbelieves, and is seen in this verse in the portion which reads: '...and (that) the verdict (of condemnation) be justified against the disbelievers,' is something which has been repeated in the Quran, such as where Allah ﷻ states: "And those who disbelieve will be driven to Hell in multitudes, until when they reach it, its gates will be opened

---

﴿...اسْتَجِيبُوا لِلَّهِ وَلِلرَّسُولِ إِذَا دَعَاكُمْ لِمَا يُحْيِيكُمْ...﴾

[60] Quran, Sūrah al-Baqarah (2), Verse 179:

﴿وَلَكُمْ فِي الْقِصَاصِ حَيَاةٌ...﴾

[61] Quran, Sūrah Yāsīn (36), Verse 70:

﴿لِيُنْذِرَ مَنْ كَانَ حَيًّا...﴾

[62] *Tafsīr Nūr al-Thaqalayn.*

and its keepers will say to them: 'Did there not come to you Messengers from among yourselves, reciting the verses of your Lord and warning you about the meeting of this Day of yours?' They will say: 'Yes (they did come), but the punishment has come into effect against the disbelievers.'"[63]

The warnings of the Quran take their source from the Knowledge of Allah ﷻ; and these warnings are of several types, however, at the crux of it:

1. They are well known and full of wisdom.
2. They are accompanied by glad tidings and innovative ways of gratification.
3. They are accompanied by visual examples on Earth which can be seen in time.

The warner which is mentioned in this verse – *'liyundhira'* – can be considered as being the Quran itself; or it can also be the Noble Prophet ﷺ, as was mentioned in the previous verse.

Take Away Messages

1. The warnings of the Quran are provided to be a source of reminder and caution for the people.

---

[63] Quran, Sūrah al-Zumar (39), Verse 71:

﴿وَسِيقَ ٱلَّذِينَ كَفَرُوٓاْ إِلَىٰ جَهَنَّمَ زُمَرًا ۖ حَتَّىٰٓ إِذَا جَآءُوهَا فُتِحَتْ أَبْوَٰبُهَا وَقَالَ لَهُمْ خَزَنَتُهَآ
أَلَمْ يَأْتِكُمْ رُسُلٌ مِّنكُمْ يَتْلُونَ عَلَيْكُمْ ءَايَٰتِ رَبِّكُمْ وَيُنذِرُونَكُمْ لِقَآءَ يَوْمِكُمْ
هَٰذَا ۚ قَالُواْ بَلَىٰ وَلَٰكِنْ حَقَّتْ كَلِمَةُ ٱلْعَذَابِ عَلَى ٱلْكَٰفِرِينَ ۝٧١﴾

2. The sign of a spiritually enlivened heart is the ability to accept the warnings of Allah ﷻ as mentioned in the Quran.
3. Accepting the guidance of the Quran is not limited to a particular community, race, or nationality. Rather, it is for all of humanity at any time and place.
4. The goal of Divine revelation *(Waḥī)* and the appointment *(Bi'that)* of the Prophets is to awaken and alert the enlivened hearts of people and complete the argument for those whose hearts are on the verge of spiritual death.
5. Even the Words of Allah ﷻ will have no impact on those who are spiritually hard-hearted.
6. The disbelievers *(kuffār)* and those who refuse to accept the Truth are nothing less than 'spiritually dead individuals' – as Allah ﷻ mentions the term 'disbelievers' as being opposite to the term 'those who have spiritual life.'
7. The promise of the wrath from the Divine for the disbelievers is something definite from Allah ﷻ.

Part 33: The Cattle: A Sign of Allah – Verse 71

أَوَ لَمْ يَرَوْا أَنَّا خَلَقْنَا لَهُم مِّمَّا عَمِلَتْ أَيْدِينَآ أَنْعَـٰمًا فَهُمْ لَهَا مَـٰلِكُونَ ﴿٧١﴾

71. Do they not see that We have created for them from what Our hands have made, cattle of which they are the masters (now).

Thinking Points

In this verse and others which will follow, Allah ﷻ once again points to the issue of Monotheism, and its opposite, polytheism.

While enumerating some of the signs of the Greatness of Allah ﷻ in the lives of His creations, and the fact that He has provided everything we need to live on this Earth, He also alludes to the inherent weakness of the idols which some choose to follow. In a clear comparison, Allah ﷻ is revealing to humanity the truth of Monotheism and the invalidity of polytheism through such subtle examples of creation.

Take Away Messages

1. For an individual to recognize the Power of Allah ﷻ, they should look at the various creations which are all around them.

2. Four-legged animals, such as cows, sheep, camels, etc., have been created for human beings. We are not obligated to be vegans or vegetarians or stay away from leather products – on the contrary, we are fully permitted to make use of these if we do not abuse the animals and follow the rules of maintaining the animals and caring for them until their slaughter.

3. Human beings play a vital role when it comes to the growth of plants and fruits as the Quran says: "So that they may eat its fruit, and (enjoy) that which their hands have worked for."[64] However, when it comes to the creation of the animals, human beings play no direct role in this as can be seen in this verse.

4. The power of creation which Allah ﷻ has is one which is innovative and is not based on imitation.

5. The sun, vegetation, rivers, and other such things are for everyone including the animal kingdom to benefit from. However, when it comes to animals, it is only human beings who fully make use of them. Yes, it is true that some animals eat other animals, however, when a human kills an animal, it is not only the meat which gets used, rather the hide is used for clothing, furniture, and in some cases, for housing such as tents. Other parts of the animal such as bones are used, as in the past, to create tools or

[64] Quran, Sūrah Yāsīn (36), Verse 35:

﴿لِيَأْكُلُوا مِن ثَمَرِهِۦ وَمَا عَمِلَتْهُ أَيْدِيهِمْ ۖ أَفَلَا يَشْكُرُونَ ﴿٣٥﴾﴾

other uses, and sometimes would even be grounded up and used in food production.

6. One of the signs of the Grace of Allah ﷻ is the fact that even though human beings play no role in the creation of animals, however, they are very easily able to dominate over them and use them for their needs.

7. The principle of ownership is something which Islam accepts. Allah ﷻ is the true Owner of everything, however, He has given others limited ownership.

Part 34: Animals: In our Service – Verses 72-73

وَذَلَّلْنَٰهَا لَهُمْ فَمِنْهَا رَكُوبُهُمْ وَمِنْهَا يَأْكُلُونَ ﴿٧٢﴾ وَلَهُمْ فِيهَا مَنَٰفِعُ
وَمَشَارِبُ ۚ أَفَلَا يَشْكُرُونَ ﴿٧٣﴾

72. And We have subdued these (cattle) for their use and benefit, so that some of them they ride, and some of them they eat.

73. And for them therein are (other) benefits and drinks, so will they still not be grateful?

Thinking Points

Continuing from the discussion in the previous verse, in the verses under review, Allah ﷻ broadens the scope of how society makes use of animals.

We know that for a large segment of people around the world, their clothing is made from some part of an animal – even if it is something small. It could be something like the wool of a sheep, or a jacket made from the hide of a cow. In addition, people around the world use animal skin for other things such as flooring, blankets, shoes, bags, wallets, and much more.

The meat and other parts of the animal may go into the food chain, and factories will process animal skins, and produce other items that people use in everyday life, so little of the animal goes to waste.

In addition, we see that the role of animals in agriculture is also very important, such as for plowing, pulling water from the wells in developing regions, providing natural fertilizers, carrying loads, and harvesting crops – and these are just some of the benefits which we get from animals.

Thus, when Allah ﷻ says that they (meaning human beings) use them for various specific purposes and then mentions that there are other benefits as well, we need to reflect on all the ways we make use of this creation of Allah ﷻ and ensure that we do not abuse them or waste this resource given to us.

Take Away Messages

1. If we could not domesticate animals such as cows and sheep, then we would not have been able to make use of the dairy products which we derive from them.
2. If all animals which Allah ﷻ has provided us with were deemed to be wild animals, then people who use them for transportation and other daily domestic uses would not have been able to travel or do tasks which require extra strength that an animal can provide.

3. Not only is the Earth tranquil and restrained,[65] but we see that even animals are the same.[66] However, it is human beings – who despite being a creation which needs both (tranquility and restraining), and so much more – is disobedient and transgresses.[67]

4. Everything Allah ﷻ creates has a purpose – nothing He does is in vain.

5. Vegetarianism or veganism is not something which has been endorsed by Islam. We have the permission and blessings of Allah ﷻ and the fourteen immaculate guides عليهم السلام to eat from the lawful animals that He has provided us with, but with certain conditions, limitations, and recommendations which we must study and follow.

6. Milk is a special blessing which we have been given, and we must show our thanks to Allah ﷻ for this. Although milk is one of the benefits we derive from animals, however, in these verses we see that Allah ﷻ did not actually mention it by name. Rather, He stated that there

---

[65] Quran, Sūrah al-Mulk (67), Verse 15:

﴿هُوَ ٱلَّذِى جَعَلَ لَكُمُ ٱلْأَرْضَ ذَلُولًا فَٱمْشُوا۟ فِى مَنَاكِبِهَا وَكُلُوا۟ مِن رِّزْقِهِۦ ۖ وَإِلَيْهِ ٱلنُّشُورُ﴾

[66] See the verse under review.

[67] Quran, Sūrah al-ʿAlaq (96), Verse 6:

﴿كَلَّآ إِنَّ ٱلْإِنسَـٰنَ لَيَطْغَىٰٓ﴾

is something we drink which comes from the animals, and as such, simply conveys one of its characteristics.

7. Thanking Allah عز وجل and those who give us benefits must be done according to one's own ability of understanding and cognizance of what they have done for us. To 'under-thank' someone – either a person or Allah عز وجل for what they do for us is unfair; just as 'over-praising' someone is not right; but obviously, we can never 'over-praise' Allah عز وجل for all that He has done for us, and we can never fully appreciate all He has done and given to us.

Part 35: Worship of Other than Allah – Verses 74-76

وَٱتَّخَذُوا۟ مِن دُونِ ٱللَّهِ ءَالِهَةً لَّعَلَّهُمْ يُنصَرُونَ ﴿٧٤﴾ لَا يَسْتَطِيعُونَ
نَصْرَهُمْ وَهُمْ لَهُمْ جُندٌ مُّحْضَرُونَ ﴿٧٥﴾ فَلَا يَحْزُنكَ قَوْلُهُمْ إِنَّا نَعْلَمُ مَا
يُسِرُّونَ وَمَا يُعْلِنُونَ ﴿٧٦﴾

74. (In spite of all this) They have taken besides Allah (false) deities (thinking) that perhaps they will be helped (by them).

75. These (false deities) cannot help them. On the contrary, they will be a host (of rebels) brought (before the Almighty receives their due punishment).

76. So let not their words grieve you (Muḥammad ﷺ). Verily, We know what they conceal and what they profess (and they will be paid back accordingly).

Thinking Points

The Quran now changes its focus on the polytheists and their state and reminds us about their invalid and unfounded thoughts. These weak individuals who cannot even defend their family, friends, and tribe think that they can stand up to Allah ﷻ – the One who has provided them with countless blessings and bounties?

Sometimes, the polytheists would run to their idols to seek respect and honour: "They have taken deities apart from

Allah so that they may be (a means of) might and glory for them."[68]

At other times, they run to their idols hoping to have them act as intercessors with the One True God – Allah ﷻ: "They worship, apart from Allah, things or beings that can neither harm, nor benefit them, and they say: 'These are our intercessors with Allah.' Say: 'Would you inform Allah of something in the heavens or the earth that He does not know? All-Glorified is He and absolutely Exalted above all that they associate with Him.'"[69]

In any case, all of these thoughts which the polytheists have about Allah ﷻ are mere mirages in their minds, and just as the Quran reiterates: "And they (the associated gods) will have no power to give them (who associate partners with Allah) any help, nor can they help themselves (as they will themselves perish)."[70]

---

[68] Quran, Sūrah Maryam (19), Verse 81:

﴿وَٱتَّخَذُوا۟ مِن دُونِ ٱللَّهِ ءَالِهَةً لِّيَكُونُوا۟ لَهُمْ عِزًّا ٨١﴾

[69] Quran, Sūrah Yūnus (10), Verse 18:

﴿وَيَعْبُدُونَ مِن دُونِ ٱللَّهِ مَا لَا يَضُرُّهُمْ وَلَا يَنفَعُهُمْ وَيَقُولُونَ هَٰٓؤُلَآءِ شُفَعَٰٓؤُنَا عِندَ ٱللَّهِ ۚ
قُلْ أَتُنَبِّـُٔونَ ٱللَّهَ بِمَا لَا يَعْلَمُ فِى ٱلسَّمَٰوَٰتِ وَلَا فِى ٱلْأَرْضِ ۚ سُبْحَٰنَهُۥ وَتَعَٰلَىٰ عَمَّا
يُشْرِكُونَ ١٨﴾

[70] Quran, Sūrah al-Aʿrāf (7), Verse 192:

﴿وَلَا يَسْتَطِيعُونَ لَهُمْ نَصْرًا وَلَآ أَنفُسَهُمْ يَنصُرُونَ ١٩٢﴾

How sad of a state these people will be in on the Day of Judgement when they are standing in ranks, with their false-gods leading them on towards the One True God – Allah ﷻ. They will be presented in the Court of Justice of Allah ﷻ, and after having lived a life of submission to the idols – despite having been given the chance to follow the Prophets and Messengers sent by Allah ﷻ – they still decided to reject them. Thus, they will all be led into Hell – not receiving the slightest bit of help from their idols.

In the final verse of review in this section, we see a form of consolation being given to Prophet Muḥammad ﷺ to further strengthen his spiritual resolve in the face of the opposition he was experiencing from the hard-headed polytheists of Mecca, and the obstacles they were placing in his way through their words and deeds. Allah ﷻ reminds His final Messenger ﷺ that he should not let the words of the polytheists sadden him. Sometimes, they called him a poet, often they referred to him as an enchant, and various times they made other accusations against him. However, Allah ﷻ sees and hears everything they say and do, and He will hold them to account.

Allah ﷻ is reminding Prophet Muḥammad ﷺ and the Muslims that neither their evil intentions towards Him are hidden, nor their secret conspiracies, denials, and overt mischief are concealed. As Allah ﷻ is All-Powerful, He confirms that He knows them all, and that He is keeping their account for the Day of Reckoning, and that the Prophet ﷺ and the Muslims will remain safe from their harm.

Upon careful reflection of this verse, we must note that it is not only Prophet Muḥammad ﷺ who found solace in this

Divine statement. Rather, every believer who goes through the difficulties of life due to religion or faces incessant attacks from the disbelievers due to their strict adherence to Islam needs to read this verse and take comfort in it.

This verse reminds us that everything is in the presence of the Almighty, and nothing will escape Him from the shrouded snares of the enemies – whether they act in the open, or in secret. Allah ﷻ promises that He will not leave His friends alone in difficult moments, and that He will **always** be there to support and protect them.

Take Away Messages

1. Associating others with Allah ﷻ and engaging in any form of idol-worshipping is equivalent to denying the blessings of Allah ﷻ.
2. One of the main reasons why people gravitate towards idol-worshipping is false understandings of the nature of Allah ﷻ and individual opinions of what they feel God should be. This leads people to create their own gods to worship, or to follow ideologies that promote the worship of multiple gods.
3. When speaking with those who have been misguided from the path of Allah ﷻ, we must show them the source of their erroneous beliefs. Once they understand that the source of what they follow is tainted and has been corrupted, then they will be able to search for the pure path towards the One and only deity worthy of worship – Allah ﷻ.

4. The punishment for those who go towards idol-worshipping, rather than taking the time to study the blessings of Allah ﷻ and thank Him, is that they will be brought forth on the Day of Judgement, being made to account for their transgressions and will then be made to go towards the fire of Hell.

5. Even the Prophets who were sent by Allah ﷻ need strengthening of their spirits, thus Allah ﷻ Himself gives them consolation during their Prophetic mission.

6. Anyone who sets admirable goals for themselves will find that people of all strata will begin to work against them to bring them down. Such righteous people will find even more obstacles and difficulties in their way that they must navigate through.

7. Focusing on the Knowledge and Awareness of Allah ﷻ as it relates to the life of an individual is one of the best ways to gain tranquility – and it is also one of the best ways to warn those who have slipped from the path of guidance.

8. The enemies plan both behind closed doors and in the open, but Allah ﷻ is Ever-Knowing of what they do and say, and He will ensure that their nefarious ways are rendered invalid.

Part 36: Signs of Allah all Around Us – Verses 77-80

أَوَلَمْ يَرَ ٱلْإِنسَٰنُ أَنَّا خَلَقْنَٰهُ مِن نُّطْفَةٍ فَإِذَا هُوَ خَصِيمٌ مُّبِينٌ ٧٧
وَضَرَبَ لَنَا مَثَلًا وَنَسِىَ خَلْقَهُۥ ۖ قَالَ مَن يُحْىِ ٱلْعِظَٰمَ وَهِىَ رَمِيمٌ ٧٨
قُلْ يُحْيِيهَا ٱلَّذِىٓ أَنشَأَهَآ أَوَّلَ مَرَّةٍ ۖ وَهُوَ بِكُلِّ خَلْقٍ عَلِيمٌ ٧٩ ٱلَّذِى
جَعَلَ لَكُم مِّنَ ٱلشَّجَرِ ٱلْأَخْضَرِ نَارًا فَإِذَآ أَنتُم مِّنْهُ تُوقِدُونَ ٨٠

77. Does a human being not see how We created them out of a (very insignificant) sperm drop? Then behold, they are an open adversary (to Us).

78. And they present for Us an example and forget their (own) creation. They say: 'Who will give life to the (dead) bones when they are decayed?'

79. Say: 'He Who gave them life the first time will again raise them to life; and He is of all creations, All-Knowing.

80. '(It is) He Who produces fire for you out of the green tree, that you kindle (another fire) from it.'

Thinking Points

It has been mentioned in various books of *Tafsīr* of the Quran that a man from the polytheists, either Ubay ibn Khalaf, Umayyah ibn Khalaf, or ʿĀṣ ibn Wāʾil found a decayed bone fragment and said to himself: "With this strong proof, I will confront Muḥammad and refute his argument about the concept of Resurrection."

He took the bone fragment and went to the Prophet of Islam ﷺ and said: "Who can bring these decayed bones back to life?" (Perhaps he also took some of the bone, crushed it into dust in the presence of the Prophet ﷺ and scattered it on the ground), then proceeded to ask Prophet Muḥammad ﷺ: "Which intellect would believe in such an event taking place?"

In response, Allah ﷻ revealed verses 77-83 of Sūrah Yāsīn and the four verses that follow, totaling seven verses, providing a logical and convincing response to people who deny or doubt the physical aspect of the Day of Resurrection.

We must appreciate the fact that Allah ﷻ created us in our first creation from nothing, and this is a decisive proof of the possibility of resurrection.

As we see, discussions related to the origin, resurrection, and Prophethood are raised in different sections of Sūrah Yāsīn – the heart of the Quran. This chapter began with the issue of Prophethood and concludes with verses that contain some of the strongest statements about the resurrection.

The Quran takes the reader by the hand and transports them back to the beginning of their life when they were nothing but a worthless drop of semen. Allah ﷻ invites an individual to contemplate and asks: "Does the person not remember that We created them from a mere sperm, yet after they become a strong, powerful, intelligent, and articulate being, they dare to dispute and openly challenge their Lord!?"

What a vivid and expressive interpretation!

First, it relies on the term 'human' which includes every individual with any belief, ideology, or level of knowledge, as anyone can comprehend the reality of their creation.

Then it speaks about the 'drop of semen,' which refers to an insignificant and worthless excretion from the male.

The Quran urges this arrogant and self-satisfied human being to reflect a little and understand what they were before they were even a fetus in the womb of their mother – they were nothing but a drop of sperm in their father's loins!

Indeed, even this insignificant drop of sperm was not the person's origin, but rather, a very tiny living cell that cannot even be seen with the naked eye, which combined with thousands of other cells floating in that drop of sperm that then made its way into the womb of a woman, looking to fertilize the egg. Eventually, from that minuscule drop, human beings took their first step into existence!

The stages of embryonic growth were traversed one after another, as mentioned in the other verses of Sūrah al-Mu'minūn where Allah ﷻ says: "We created humankind (in the very beginning) from a specially sifted extract of clay. Then We made it into a fertilized ovum in a safe lodging. Then We created of the fertilized ovum a clot clinging (to the womb wall), and (afterwards in sequence) We created of the clinging clot a (chew of) lump, and We created of (a chew of) lump bones, and We clothed the bones in flesh. Then We caused it to grow into another creation. So Blessed and Supreme is Allah, the Creator Who creates everything in the best and most appropriate form and has the ultimate rank of creativity. Then, after all this, you are bound to die.

Thereafter, you will, on the Day of Resurrection, certainly be raised up."[71]

After birth, when the infant was weak and helpless, it quickly passed through the stages of development until it reached physical and intellectual maturity and growth.

Indeed, this weak and helpless being became so strong and powerful that it allowed itself to engage in aggression against the call of Allah ﷻ, forgetting its past and future, becoming an example of being a "clear and open adversary."

Interestingly, the interpretation of being a "clear adversary" has both a strong aspect and a weak aspect, and apparently the Quran refers to both directions.

On the one hand, this act is from a being who possesses intellect, thought, consciousness, independent will, choice, and power. We know that the most important characteristic which only human beings have out of millions of creations is the ability to speak and articulate themselves.

However, on the other hand, it is a forgetful and arrogant creature who uses the blessings bestowed upon it against itself, engaging in arguments and conflicts – what an unaware and bewildered being the human is!

---

[71] Quran, Sūrah al-Mu'minūn (23), Verses 12-16:

﴿وَلَقَدْ خَلَقْنَا ٱلْإِنسَٰنَ مِن سُلَٰلَةٍ مِّن طِينٍ ١٢ ثُمَّ جَعَلْنَٰهُ نُطْفَةً فِى قَرَارٍ مَّكِينٍ ١٣ ثُمَّ
خَلَقْنَا ٱلنُّطْفَةَ عَلَقَةً فَخَلَقْنَا ٱلْعَلَقَةَ مُضْغَةً فَخَلَقْنَا ٱلْمُضْغَةَ عِظَٰمًا فَكَسَوْنَا ٱلْعِظَٰمَ
لَحْمًا ثُمَّ أَنشَأْنَٰهُ خَلْقًا ءَاخَرَ فَتَبَارَكَ ٱللَّهُ أَحْسَنُ ٱلْخَٰلِقِينَ ١٤ ثُمَّ إِنَّكُم بَعْدَ ذَٰلِكَ
لَمَيِّتُونَ ١٥ ثُمَّ إِنَّكُمْ يَوْمَ ٱلْقِيَٰمَةِ تُبْعَثُونَ ١٦﴾

For their ignorance, it is enough that the Quran states that such people make an example for us – that is, they create idols and partners for Allah – and create all reasons for their stubbornness against the One True Creator, while they themselves forgot their own initial creation.

Interestingly, the Noble Quran gave this person who came to Prophet Muḥammad ﷺ with the bone a thorough answer with the short phrase: "...and he forgets his [own] creation."

The Quran tells this person, and all of those who hold such beliefs that: "If you had not forgotten your own creation, you would never have fallen into such futile and weak reasoning, O forgetful human! Look back and contemplate on your own creation, how insignificant you were as a mere drop of semen, and every day a fresh garment of life was placed upon you. You are constantly in a state of death and resurrection. You emerged from inanimate matter. From the world of plants and the animal kingdom, you became a human being. But you, in your forgetfulness, have brushed all this aside into the realm of oblivion. Now you ask, who can revive this decayed bone?! Indeed, who can revive this bone, when it completely decays, turns back into dirt. But you forget that you too were once dirt before Allah ﷻ created the first human being from the soil of the earth."

Therefore, immediately, Allah ﷻ commands the Prophet of Islam ﷺ to tell such rejecters that the same One Who brought that bone you hold into existence in the first place will give them life again.

If today, a decayed bone is all that remains of a person, recognize that there was a time when even this decayed bone did not exist, nor was there any earth to create them from!

The One who created this individual from non-existence can easily revive a decayed bone.

In addition, Prophet Muḥammad ﷺ is told to tell such individuals that if they think that when this decayed bone turns into dust and scatters about, who can recognize its components and gather them from various places? The answer to this is also clear that Allah ﷻ is aware of every creation and knows all their characteristics to be able to bring them back into existence.

A person who has even a basic level of knowledge and power will not find the resurrection and the revival of the dead problematic.

In addition, we should realize that not only is Allah ﷻ aware of the origin of human creation, but He is also aware of their intentions and actions, and their accounts and records are all clear before Him.

Therefore, calculating actions, intentions, and inner beliefs do not pose a problem for Him, as stated in the Quran: "To Allah belongs all that is in the heavens and the earth; whether you reveal what is within yourselves (of intentions, plans) or keep it secret, Allah will call you to account for it. He forgives whomever He Wills (either from His own Grace, or His Mercy responding to the repentance of the sinful), and He punishes whomever He Wills (as a requirement of His Justice). Allah has full Power over everything."[72]

---

[72] Quran, Sūrah al-Baqarah (2), Verse 284:

For this reason, Prophet Mūsā was commanded to respond to Pharaoh, as he too doubted the concept of Resurrection, and expressed astonishment at the resurrection of past generations and their accountability. Prophet Mūsā was told to say: "My Lord holds the knowledge of them in a Record. My Lord never errs, nor forgets."[73]

The meaning of 'tree' mentioned in this selection of verses were two specific types of wood which were used to kindle fires, namely: *markh* and *ʿafār*. The Arabs would rub these two sticks together to light a fire, just like we use matches today.[74]

Creating fire from green branches of trees has been presented so that people can understand how Allah has made something like this possible, and so the scholars and researchers could also realize that energy is stored within a tree, and through this they may come to scientific realizations.

﴿لِّلَّهِ مَا فِي ٱلسَّمَٰوَٰتِ وَمَا فِي ٱلْأَرْضِ ۗ وَإِن تُبْدُوا۟ مَا فِىٓ أَنفُسِكُمْ أَوْ تُخْفُوهُ يُحَاسِبْكُم بِهِ ٱللَّهُ ۖ فَيَغْفِرُ لِمَن يَشَآءُ وَيُعَذِّبُ مَن يَشَآءُ ۗ وَٱللَّهُ عَلَىٰ كُلِّ شَىْءٍ قَدِيرٌ ٢٨٤﴾

[73] Quran, Sūrah Ṭāhā (20), Verse 52:

﴿قَالَ عِلْمُهَا عِندَ رَبِّى فِى كِتَٰبٍ ۖ لَّا يَضِلُّ رَبِّى وَلَا يَنسَى ٥٢﴾

[74] *Tafsīr Rāhnumā.*

The Resurrection of Energies

In a follow-up from the previous verses that discussed the concept of resurrection and contained significant and vivid references to the possibility of resurrection and the elimination of any exclusion, in the verses under discussion, which are the final verses of Sūrah Yāsīn – the heart of the Quran – a more detailed and explicit description of this issue is presented, and it presents the discussion in a few interesting ways.

Firstly, it states that the same God Who created for you fire from green trees which you then use for various purposes is capable of clothing these decayed bones with the garment of life once again.

What a strange and fascinating interpretation that provides us with deeper meanings the more we delve into it!

In essence, many verses of the Quran have multiple meanings, some are simple which aid in the understanding of the public at any time and place; others are profound and are geared towards the scholars; and ultimately some are entirely profound for a specific group of individuals, and for future eras when the collective knowledge of humanity will increase.

Although the meaning of the verses of the Quran can differ based on who is reading and reflecting on them, these meanings do not contradict one another and are united in a meaningful interpretation.

The last verse in the section under review is like this.

The first interpretation that many commentators have mentioned and is a simple and clear meaning understandable to the public is as follows: In ancient times among the Arabs, it was common to use specific types of wood, such as *markh* and *'afār* to kindle fire. These types of wood were used for producing fire in which one piece of wood was placed underneath, and the other one was placed on top, and in rubbing the two types of wood together, the ancient Arabs would generate sparks, igniting a fire – like how others would use a flint stone, or how we use matches today.

In this passage of verses, the Quran reminds us that the same God Who can send forth fire from these green trees has the power to clothe the dead with the garment of life.

As we know, water and fire are two opposing elements – and thus, the One Who enabled a green branch which is moist and technically filled with 'water' to create fire is very able to bring the dead back to life and give death to the living.

Glory be to the Creator Who keeps fire within the embrace of water, and water within the embrace of fire – surely, for Him, clothing life onto the bodies of dead humans is not an arduous task.

If we go a step further in this meaning, we reach a more precise interpretation, which is that the ability to kindle a fire through wood is not exclusive to the types of wood which the Arabs referred to as *markh and 'afār*. Rather, this ability exists in all trees and all objects in the universe – although the mentioned wood types have a greater readiness for this task due to their specific properties.

In summary, if any type of wood encounters another wood in a specific fashion, they can produce fire – even wood from trees which are fresh and moist.

For this reason, sometimes massive forest fires occur where not a single human being is the cause. It could be due to intense winds and storms that force the branches of trees to rub against each other, and a spark falls among the dry leaves, and the winds pick up the smoldering leaves, making them grow into massive forest fires.

This is the same fire that resides within all particles of existence and manifest itself during friction. This broader interpretation expands the view of the combination of opposites in creation and makes eternity *(baqā)* more apparent within the concept of annihilation *(fanā')*.

As for the third interpretation which is even deeper and profound in its meaning, with the help of the knowledge of today, we refer to it as the "Resurrection of Energies."

One of the crucial functions of plants is the process of capturing carbon dioxide in the air and producing plant cellulose – cellulose being the main component of trees, consisting primarily of carbon, oxygen, and hydrogen.

The cells of trees and plants take in the carbon dioxide from the air and break it up – freeing the oxygen and retaining carbon within themselves which they combine with water to create wood.

However, the crucial point is that according to the testimony of scientists, any chemical reaction either requires the absorption of specific energy or the release of it.

Therefore, when trees are engaged in capturing carbon, according to this law, they require the presence of energy, and here they utilize heat and sunlight as an active energy source.

Thus, during the formation of tree wood, a certain amount of solar energy is also stored within them. When we burn wood, that stored solar energy is released again because carbon combines oxygen from the air, forming carbon gas, while oxygen and hydrogen are a portion of water.

To put it very simple, the cozy warmth and light that fill the cottage in the winter, or the glow of a coal fire are the same warmth and light of the sun that have been stored within these items for several years or decades, and what the tree gradually received from the sun throughout its lifetime, it now gives back without any loss!

Here, we reach the topic of the resurrection of energy and see that the scattered light and heat in this space caresses and nurtures the leaves of trees and their wood. They were never destroyed; rather, they changed their form and are hidden from our eyes within particles, wood, branches, and leaves of trees.

When a flame reaches dry wood, their process of resurrection begins, and the hidden solar energy in the tree then becomes apparent, without diminishing to the extent of the brightness of a candle.

Undoubtedly, this meaning was not clear to the masses at the time of the revelation of this verse. However, as we mentioned, this does not pose any problem because the verses of the Quran have multi-layered meanings, at diverse levels, and for people of different aptitudes.

One day, they understood something from this verse, and today, we understand more, and perhaps future generations will go beyond this and comprehend even more. At the same time, all these meanings are correct, entirely acceptable, and contribute to the overall understanding of this verse.

Some questions may arise:

Why a green tree?

Sometimes it may come to mind: Why does the Quran make note of it being a green tree here, while it is difficult to ignite fire with moist wood? It would have been better to use dry wood instead, to be consistent with the interpretation given.

However, the interesting point is this: Only green trees can perform carbon fixation and store solar energy. Dry trees, even if exposed to sunlight for hundreds of years, do not add a particle to their thermal energy storage. They are only capable of this important task when they are green and alive.

Therefore, it is only the "green tree" that can provide us with fuel (ignition) for fire, and it mysteriously preserves heat and light in its cool and moist wood. However, as soon as the wood dries out, the process of carbon fixation and solar energy storage is halted.

Based on this principle, the above interpretation depicts a beautiful portrayal of the resurrection of energies, and a timeless scientific miracle from the Noble Quran.

Furthermore, if we return to the other interpretations mentioned above, the interpretation of the "green tree" remains intact. This is because when the wood of green trees experiences strong friction with each other, they produce sparks that can ignite fire. This is where we realize the greatness of the Power of Allah ﷻ in preserving fire within water and water within fire.

What is the difference between 'ignition' of fire and 'kindling' of fire?

1. The word *'tūqidūn'* which is used in the verse means 'lighting a fire with fuel.'
2. The word *'īqād'* means 'igniting a fire.'
3. The word *'waqūd'* means 'a fuel used for kindling a fire.'

Therefore, the phrase "That you kindle another fire from it," refers to the kindling of fire using those fuels, and in another interpretation, it refers to 'igniting' rather than 'kindling' a fire.

Therefore, the Quran says: "That is the God who has provided you with fire from the green tree, and you kindle fire with it (not ignite fire). He can bring the dead back to life," and this interpretation is perfectly aligned with the resurrection of energies.

In any case, the matter of igniting fire with tree wood, although it seems simple to us, becomes apparent with careful consideration that it is one of the most amazing phenomena in our world. The materials that make up a tree, with a massive portion being water and some components from the earth, none of which are flammable. What power has created this energy-generating substance from water, soil, and air that has been linked to human life for thousands of years?

Take Away Messages

1. If people could keep their own personal weaknesses in mind and remain humble, then no one would ever be proud or arrogant.

2. By focusing on the fact that we have been created from an insignificant drop of sperm – literally, we have come from nothing, and our faith in the Day of Resurrection, and that Allah ﷻ can resurrect us and recreate us just as He created us from nothing, should be strengthened.
3. Even worse than a person having the roots of hostility within them is when that raging anger is done in the open.
4. Conflict between a human being and Allah ﷻ is something which is not expected, and for this reason, in verse 77, the word "إِذَا" has been used which refers to those actions that a person does which are unexpected.
5. It is permissible for a person to convey the incorrect beliefs that exist in a society if their aim is to respond intellectually to erroneous beliefs which are creeping into the public.
6. The primary source for most of the disputes concerning the Power of Allah ﷻ lies in not paying attention to similar examples which are present all around us and forgetting the past.
7. Those who deny resurrection do so with no proof whatsoever – all they have is their own arrogance.
8. Intellectual freedom in Islam is such that even those who deny Allah ﷻ and the Day of Resurrection can stand in the presence of the leader of the Muslims – the Prophet ﷺ in this case – and clearly speak their mind with no repercussions.

9. There is no problem in asking questions about religion – that which is looked down upon is disrespectful and ill-mannered motives for questioning.
10. The source of some of the theological doubts is when people begin to draw comparisons between the power of human beings and the Power of Allah ﷻ.
11. Theological doubts must be responded to – even if it is only one person raising such doubts because if not dealt with on time, then that one individual may knowingly or unknowingly misguide others.
12. The resurrection of humanity is a physical event.
13. Resurrection is reliant upon two things: One is the Power of Allah ﷻ in recreating human beings; and the other is His Knowledge of humanity's past actions. The Quran shows us that He has both abilities: "He Who gave them life the first time," shows the Power of Allah ﷻ; and "He is of all creations, All-Knowing," shows His infinite Knowledge.
14. Allah ﷻ often draws parallels between opposites in the Quran; for example, water and fire are two entities which can never be in harmony with one another, but He brings both in this verse.

Part 37: The Creator of Everything – Verse 81

أَوَلَيْسَ ٱلَّذِى خَلَقَ ٱلسَّمَٰوَٰتِ وَٱلْأَرْضَ بِقَٰدِرٍ عَلَىٰٓ أَن يَخْلُقَ مِثْلَهُمۚ
بَلَىٰ وَهُوَ ٱلْخَلَّٰقُ ٱلْعَلِيمُ ٨١

81. Is He Who created the heavens and the earth, not able to create likes of them? Yes, indeed; and He is the Supreme Creator, (and) the All-Knowing.

Thinking Points

The human being is a combination of both a physical body and an immaterial spirit – the physical body of the human being will perish with death, and even while alive, it continuously goes through changes; however, the soul and character of a person are immutable. On the Day of Judgement, the soul of a human being will be the same soul which one had in this transient world; however, the physical body of the person will be a form which is **like** the physical body which one had while in the transient world, but not the exact same.

Take Away Messages

1. There are times when a person must respond to the questions of people, and they cannot remain silent.

2. Questions are one way in which the sleeping consciousness of a person can be revived.

3. When speaking to those who deny Allah ﷻ, we should always start with minor issues and then work our way up to the larger, more detailed, and important subjects. In this chapter, we see that Allah ﷻ first starts by talking about the fertilized egg; and from there He brings forth the example of a green, living tree; then in the third example, He speaks about the creation of the universe.

4. A Persian proverb says: *'Since we have reached 100, it means that we first arrived at 90'* – meaning that the One Who created the entire universe and the Earth, can also create the human being.

5. Allah ﷻ can create anything, anywhere He wills – whether it be here in this temporal world, or in the world to come on the Day of Resurrection, or beyond that.

6. In addition to the Wisdom and Justice of Allah ﷻ being proof of the resurrection, His Power and Knowledge over the actions of all of humanity also act as proof for the Day of Accounting.

Part 38: Be and It Is – Verses 82-83

إِنَّمَآ أَمۡرُهُۥٓ إِذَآ أَرَادَ شَيۡـًٔا أَن يَقُولَ لَهُۥ كُن فَيَكُونُ ﴿٨٢﴾ فَسُبۡحَٰنَ
ٱلَّذِي بِيَدِهِۦ مَلَكُوتُ كُلِّ شَيۡءٖ وَإِلَيۡهِ تُرۡجَعُونَ ﴿٨٣﴾

82. Verily, His command when He intends a thing is (only) that He says to it: 'Be' and it is (that comes into being).

83. Therefore, Glory be to Him in Whose hands is the dominion of all things, and to Him you will be returned.

Thinking Points

Since faith in the Day of Resurrection must be firmly engrained within the believer, any doubts must be answered in such a way that not a single ounce of uncertainty remains.

As we recall from a previous section, in response to the individual who brought a decayed bone to the Prophet ﷺ, crushed it, threw it to the ground, then asked how it can be brought back to life again, Allah ﷻ responded to his question with multiple answers, the final one of them being what we see in this verse under review where Allah says: "Verily, His command, when He intends a thing, is (only) that He says to it: 'Be' and it is."

The fulfillment of His command and the Divine Will does not require **any** time at all to take place – technically, it can be referred to happening in even less than 'the blinking of an eye' as we see in the Quran: "And Our command is (at once carried out by) only one (word) like the twinkling of an eye."[75]

Allah ﷻ does not even need to say the word – *"kun"* translated as "Be!" If He had to utter even this word then He would be in some need, and this is far beyond His status to have to do so. Therefore, the meaning of the word *"kun"* translated as "Be!" is merely an intention and order of Allah ﷻ. According to Imam ʿAlī ؑ: "[He creates] but not with a voice which cries out, nor with a call that is heard."[76]

Take Away Messages

1. It is easy for Allah ﷻ to create anything and everything.
2. In creating the world of existence, Allah ﷻ is neither in need of a means, nor help, and no one can prevent Him from doing anything that He Wills.
3. There is no interruption between the intention of Allah ﷻ and the actualization of that act.
4. How is it even possible for people to presume that Allah ﷻ is incapable of bringing about the Day of Resurrection? He is free from all limitations and inabilities.

---

[75] Quran, Sūrah al-Qamar (54), Verse 50:

﴿وَمَا أَمْرُنَا إِلَّا وَاحِدَةٌ كَلَمْحٍ بِالْبَصَرِ﴾

[76] *Nahj al-Balāgha*, Sermon 186:

لَا بِصَوْتٍ يَقْرَعُ وَلَا بِنِدَاءٍ يُسْمَعُ.

5. Not only is the source of all things in His proverbial hands, but everything will also return to Him.

Conclusion by the Translator

Shaykh Muḥsin Qarā'atī's commentary of Sūrah Yāsīn offers a rich and multi-dimensional exploration of one of the most revered chapters in the Quran.

His research took us through theological themes, ethical teachings, and practical lessons, all while drawing deeply from the powerful structure and eloquent arguments which Allah ﷻ brought forth within the eighty-three verses.

Sūrah Yāsīn began with compelling support of the truthfulness of the call of Prophet Muḥammad ﷺ and the clarity of his mission, grounding its audience in the necessity of revelation and the call to righteousness.

This initial declaration was more than just an introduction to this chapter; it was a direct invitation to self-examination about one's own alignment with the "Straight Path" brought by the Prophet of Islam ﷺ.

A central motif of the commentary was its narration of historical events and stories, notably the account of the three messengers and the lone believer in a disbelieving community. These stories are not mere historical records, but instructive case studies. They underscore the Quranic principle that the human response to Divine guidance – whether it be faith and acceptance, or denial and mockery – shapes the fate of individuals and societies.

Shaykh Qarā'atī also highlights the barriers to faith that people construct, including arrogance, societal pressures, and the illusion of self-sufficiency. Through his commentary, he encourages readers to identify and dismantle these inner obstacles, recognizing that denying faith is often a matter of deliberate rejection, rather than genuine lack of understanding. This theme ties closely to the broader Quranic focus on sincerity and openness to the truth.

The commentary of Sūrah Yāsīn continually reinforces the concept of ultimate accountability: every deed is recorded, and every soul will be judged perfectly on the Day of Judgement. The vivid, sometimes startling, depictions of the afterlife instill both hope for Paradise, and fear of Hell – guiding believers to live with a sense of responsibility and anticipation for their final return to Allah ﷻ.

Appreciation of Allah's ﷻ signs in creation forms another major pillar of this chapter. The cycles of life and death, the wonders of nature, and the regularity of cosmic phenomena are all presented as unmistakable affirmations of Divine Power and Providence. The reader was repeatedly nudged to look beyond the surface and develop an ongoing, reflective relationship with the world to strengthen gratitude, humility, and faith.

Practical, religious, and social guidance is woven throughout the commentary, with special attention on charity, wise use of resources, compassion for others, and the futility of idol worshipping and superstitions. In short, we learned that genuine spirituality must translate into upright action and concern for others, not just ritual observance.

Through structured "thinking points" and clear "take away messages," each section of the commentary sought to ground spiritual insights in daily relevance, helping readers internalize lessons and live more purposefully.

In closing, this work upholds Sūrah Yāsīn as a call to mindful, grateful, and ethical living – rooted in unwavering faith, and persistent reflection on the realities of life, death, and the eternal Hereafter.

This monumental work of Shaykh Muḥsin Qarā'atī invites readers to remain steadfast on the Straight Path – ever conscious of both Allah's عزّ وجلّ Infinite Mercy and Perfect Justice.

الحمد لله رب العالمين

Other Publications Available[77]

1. *A Land Most Goodly: The Story of Yemen in the Quran and in the Times of Prophet Muḥammad and Imam ʿAlī ibn Abī Ṭālib,* by Jaffer Ladak
2. *A Star Amongst the Stars: The Life and Times of the Great Companion: Jabir ibn Abdullah al-Ansari,* by Jaffer Ladak*
3. *Alif, Baa, Taa of Kerbala,* by Saleem Bhimji and Arifa Hudda
4. *Arbāʿīn of Imam Ḥusayn,* compiled and translated by Saleem Bhimji
5. *Daily Devotions,* compiled and translated by Saleem Bhimji*
6. *Deficient? A Review of Sermon 80 from Nahj al-Balāgha,* by Āyatullāh al-ʿUẓmā Shaykh Nāṣir Makārim Shīrāzī and translated by Saleem Bhimji
7. *Exegesis of the 29th Juz of the Quran a Translation of Tafsīr Nemunah,* by Āyatullāh al-ʿUẓmā Shaykh Nāṣir Makārim Shīrāzī and translated by Saleem Bhimji*
8. *Foundations of Islamic Unity* a translation of *Al-Fuṣūl al-Muhimmah fī Ta'līf al-Ummah,* by ʿAbd al-Ḥusayn Sharaf al-Dīn al-Mūsawī al-ʿĀmilī and translated by Batool

[77] The following is a list of all the original writings and translations from the Islamic Publishing House. As many of these titles are out of stock, we are slowly re-releasing all our works via Print-on-Demand through Amazon.

Titles with an * after the name are currently available via Amazon from their international platforms, including Australia, Canada, France, Germany, Italy, Japan, UK, USA, Netherlands, and Spain.

If you cannot find any of the above titles on Amazon, feel free to email us at **iph@iph.ca**.

Ispahany*

9. *Fountain of Paradise: Fāṭima az-Zahrā᾽ in the Noble Quran,* by Āyatullāh al-ʿUẓmā Shaykh Nāṣir Makārim Shīrāzī, compiled and translated by Saleem Bhimji*
10. *God and god of Science,* by Syed Hasan Raza Jafri*
11. *House of Sorrows,* by Shaykh ʿAbbās al-Qummī and translated by Aejaz Ali Turab Husayn Husayni*
12. *Iʿtikāf: The Spiritual Retreat – The Philosophy, Spiritual Mysteries and Practical Rulings,* compiled and translated by Saleem Bhimji*
13. *Inspirational Insights,* by Mohammed Khaku
14. *Islam and Religious Pluralism,* by Āyatullāh Shaykh Murtaḍā Muṭahharī and translated by Sayyid Sulayman Ali Hasan
15. *Journey to Eternity – A Handbook of Supplications for the Soul,* compiled and translated by Saleem Bhimji and Arifa Hudda*
16. *Love and Hate for Allah's Sake,* by Mujtaba Saburi translated by Saleem Bhimji
17. *Love for the Family,* compiled and translated by Yasin T. Al-Jibouri, Saleem Bhimji, and others*
18. *Moral Management,* by Abbas Rahimi and translated by Saleem Bhimji*
19. *Morals of the Masumeen,* by Arifa Hudda
20. *Prayers of the Final Prophet – A Collection of Supplications of Prophet Muḥammad,* by ʿAllāmah Sayyid Muḥammad Ḥusayn Ṭabā᾽ṭabā᾽ī and translated by Tahir Ridha-Jaffer*
21. *Prospering Through a Cost of Living Crisis,* by Jaffer Ladak*
22. *Ramaḍān Reflections,* compiled by A Group of Muslim

Scholars and translated by Saleem Bhimji*

23. *Ṣalāt al-Āyāt,* by Saleem Bhimji
24. *Ṣalāt al-Ghufaylah: Salvation through Patience & Perseverance,* written by Saleem Bhimji*
25. *Secrets of the Ḥajj,* by Āyatullāh al-ʿUẓmā Shaykh Ḥusayn Mazāherī and translated by Saleem Bhimji
26. *Sunan an-Nabī,* by ʿAllāmah Sayyid Muḥammad Ḥusayn Ṭabāʾṭabāʾī and translated by Tahir Ridha-Jaffer
27. *Tears from Heaven's Flowers: An Anthology of English Poetry about the Ahlulbayt,* by Abrahim al-Zubeidi
28. *The Day the Germs Caused Fitnah,* by Umm Maryam*
29. *The Firmest Armament: Commentary on Āyatul Kursī (The Verse of the Throne),* by Sayyid Nasrullah Burujerdi and translated by Saleem Bhimji*
30. *The Last Luminary and Ways to Delve into the Light,* by Sayyid Muḥammad Ridha Husayni Mutlaq and translated by Saleem Bhimji*
31. *The Muslim Legal Will Booklet,* by Saleem Bhimji*
32. *The Pure Life,* by Āyatullāh al-ʿUẓmā as-Sayyid Muḥammad Taqī al-Modarresī and translated by Jaffer Ladak with commentary by Dr. Zainali Panjwani and Jaffer Ladak*
33. *The Third Testimony: Imam ʿAlī in the Adhān,* compiled and translated by Saleem Bhimji*
34. *The Tragedy of Kerbalāʾ,* as narrated by Imam ʿAlī ibn al-Ḥusayn al-Sajjād عليه السلام, recorded by Shaykh al-Ṣadūq and translated by ʿAbdul Zahrāʾ ʿAbdul Ḥusayn*
35. *The Torch of Perpetual Guidance – A Brief Commentary on Ziyārat al-ʿĀshūrāʾ,* by ʿAbbās Azizi and translated by Saleem Bhimji

36. *Weapon of the Believer,* by ʿAllāmah Muḥammad Bāqir Majlisī and translated by Saleem Bhimji*

Upcoming Publications

1. *Beyond the 40th: Understanding the Exclusive Significance of the Arbaʿīn of Imam al-Ḥusayn* ﷵ, by the late Āyatullāh al-Sayyid Muḥammad Muḥsin Ḥusaynī Ṭehrānī, translated by Saleem Bhimji
2. *Guided By Faith: The Islamic Management Model*, written by ʿAbbās Raḥīmī, translated by Saleem Bhimji
3. *Knocking on Heaven's Doors*, compiled with translations by Saleem Bhimji
4. *Propaganda and Piety: The Umayyad Rewriting of Syria [From Historical Syria to Apocalyptic Syria]*, written by Dr. Rasūl Jaʿfariyān, translated by Saleem Bhimji
5. *Ramaḍān Devotions: A Collection of Supplications for the Nights of Qadr*, compiled with translations by Saleem Bhimji
6. *Blessed Desires: Islamic Perspectives on Sexuality and the Soul*, by ʿAlī Ḥoseinzādeh, translated by Saleem Bhimji
7. *Shadows of Dissent*, by Āyatullāh Shaykh Nāṣir Makārim Shīrāzī, translated by Saleem Bhimji and the Translator's Guild of the Islamic Publishing House
8. *Supplication for the People of the Frontiers*, by Shaykh Ḥusayn Anṣāriān, translated by Saleem Bhimji
9. *The Arbaʿīn: A look into the Ziyārat of Arbaʿīn*, written by Saleem Bhimji
10. *The Comprehensive Book of Marriage and Divorce Formulas*, by Saleem Bhimji
11. *The Young Muslims Daily Devotions Manuals – Volumes I and II*, compiled and translated by Saleem Bhimji
12. *Victor Not Victim: A Biography of Lady Zaynab binte ʿAlī*

and two hundred Short Stories, researched and written by Saleem Bhimji

13. *Weekly Spiritual Ascent: Ṣalāt al-Jumuʿah: Philosophy, Practice, and Personal Piety*, compiled and translated by Saleem Bhimji

Our *Living the Quran Through The Living Quran* series of commentary on the Noble Quran is also being published. To date, we have released the commentary of:

1. Sūrah al-Fātiḥa (1)
2. Sūrah Yāsīn (36)
3. Sūrah Qāf (50)
4. Sūrah al-Najm (53)
5. Sūrah al-Wāqiʿah (56)
6. Sūrah al-Mujādilah (58)

The commentary of the following chapters of the Quran will also be released in the future:

1. Sūrah al-Ṣaff (61)

Supporting Our Projects

If you would like to donate to any of our ongoing projects, such as our upcoming book publications, video content, or articles, you can contribute in the following ways:

Within Canada: Send an e-transfer from your Canadian bank account to **iph@iph.ca**

International: Send your transfer via PayPal to **saleem1176@rogers.com**

For more information,
check out our website:

www.iph.ca

Contact us for more information at:

iph@iph.ca